How to Avoid the Pitfalls:

Building Your Dream Home

By

Pierre Renaldo

ISBN: 0-7596-6694-6

This book is printed on acid free paper.

First published by The Freeport Company S.A., RO-610 444 Brickell Avenue, Suite #51, Miami Florida, 33131-2492

1stBooks - rev. 1/18/02

"He who does not lose his center endures"

Laotsu

Table of Contents

Introduction

What this book is about.

After forty-five years in the front lines of the construction industry, I thought it would be a good idea to share some very intimate secrets with people who are about to embark on one of the most exciting experiences of a lifetime; **building your dream home.**

Perhaps it is a retirement gift to yourself, after many years of hard work, maybe a vacation retreat. Possibly that first giant step toward building the wonderful place for family, where your kids will grow up and/or your children and grand children will come to visit, years hence.

I thought that if I shared these ideas, I could enlighten people, help them with an overview of the entire construction process, in simple detail, without a lot of technical jargon. Just an easy to read handbook, an outline that people could follow. Something useful, like a guidebook you buy to explore vacation ideas. Why not make it easy for *anybody* to understand, even if they didn't know anything about construction?

Many people are confused and discouraged by technicalities when they pick up a book that is supposed to enlighten, only to be left in complete dismay at their lack of understanding about a subject for which they crave more knowledge.

Construction of anything is a very complex undertaking, and a very technical subject. So some books written to instruct people on the finer points of construction tend to be nearly mysterious to those with little or no experience. Don't be intimidated! This book will explain the "nitty gritty" you need to know in simplistic terms that will enlighten.

There is no doubt in my mind, that you are driven to seek knowledge which will enable you to avoid experiencing the kind of horror stories you have heard. By the time you make the decision to go ahead with a construction project, you have likely been deluged with advice from friends and relatives who have taken the plunge and who kindly wish to share their disastrous experiences with anybody they can get to listen.

So then of course, it is off to the library or bookstore for you, to find just the right treatise that will instruct you in the fine arts of hand-to-hand construction combat, or guide you safely and happily through the mine fields of the actual building process. If you read enough and talk to enough people, you will know what to do, and what to expect, right? After all, knowledge is power!

It has been my experience with my clientele, that building can be fun and enjoyable if:

1.) you are well informed;
2.) you go about it with an open mind and;
3.) you have a good positive attitude. Having the right people to work with will help and I hope to assist you in finding them.

This book was written to guide you through the entire process and be happy with the end results. Not only with the product, but also the people you have been dealing with over a period of several months. In other words, your story will have a 'happy ending'.

I doubt if this book is a first, but it is intended to be a simplified guidance system to lead you around usually unforeseen and oftentimes **'avoidable problems'** and to introduce you to methods of coping with those nasty necessities you must take head on.

Who This Book Is For:

This book is for people who would like to build their dream house without getting old before their time. People who would like to avoid falling into the traps or 'pits' that seem to be the norm. But you don't have to fall into a 'pit' just because someone you know dug himself or herself into one.

I will refer to these pitfalls (*avoidable misunderstandings)*, as 'pits' throughout this book. If you are armed with the knowledge of what to expect in advance, then you will not be shocked to learn of some surprise (often in the form of unforeseen expense) that awaits you. Instead, you will be one of the anointed who can boast of a truly enjoyable adventure in building.

So many single women have related to me, the difficulties they have had to endure attempting to go it alone, that I would include them as a special category. Other people with little or no experience in building, singles and married alike, and those who would like a different slant on the home building subject, even though they have done it all before. If this book can keep you out of one 'pit', then it has been a worthwhile effort for me.

What This Book Is Not:

This is not just another "How To" book. You will not find instructions for building a fireplace or creating a basement recreation room in these pages.

There is not one single hint about hanging an overhead garage door, or how to install ceramic tile in a shower. It is not a technical journal, nor anything remotely resembling a textbook.

If you are looking for that kind of information, it is available at a nearby library or in booklet form at a local building supply company.

This book is not necessarily intended as a guide for those bold and hearty souls who want to be their own general contractor, (though for some it would serve as a useful checklist). Them I salute. If they feel confident and have had some experience in the construction industry or the trades, then they already know the routine.

The construction industry, so often maligned, has been my chosen field of endeavor, my life's work. And though I have met some unscrupulous contractors, and read about the worst and most sensational scandals in the newspapers, I believe most contractors are honest, hard working and certainly as dedicated a segment of American industry as exists in the business community today.

After all the hype over other kinds of scandals in the business world; insider stock trading; savings and loan 'failures'; junk bond swindles; embezzling by accountants and book keepers; outright thievery by lawyers; criminal neglect by health care professionals; plundering by political thugs in our most revered public offices; then I do not think the construction industry comes out looking too badly.

This book is not an expose`. I am not turning over any flat rocks. If you like that sort of 'entertainment' just turn on the TV News.

PART 1
Selecting the Site

One of the most important decisions you will make when planning a home building project is where you are going to build it. Often, this is a lengthy search, especially if you have a mental image of what you expect to find and nothing even comes close to matching your dream building site.

I'm sure you have heard the first rule of buying property. There are three very important things that should take priority in you decision making. Location! Location! Location! Let me expand on that briefly.

Good Location:

This is a relative term, because good location can mean so many different things to different people. Your real estate agent is trying to convince you that the building lot she has listed is just the thing. The 'best school in town' is just two block away, there is shopping within a quarter of a mile and the bus stop is only a few steps from 'your front door'. Now that might sound ideal for some people but it could be pure rubbish for you.

Each of us has our own idea of what good location means, and sometimes we are willing to sacrifice convenience for enchantment. The location described in the foregoing paragraph might be perfect for those who are slaves to accessibility. People who want everything at their fingertips. But you prefer the serenity of the suburbs, even more so the countryside. And when you find that perfect spot, then your location requirements have been fulfilled.

Let me assure you friends, there are multitudes of great locations if you know what to look for. I will make a few suggestions that may give you new insights into selection of your ideal building site. Then I will give you some real life examples of what I think constitutes good location.

Here are some factors for you to bear in mind and to add into your equation when you are out there looking for your perfect spot.

1

Site Access:

Will this site give you access during and after the construction process?

Will it be easy to get in and out during inclement weather?

Are there any special permits required for driveways, or curb cuts?

Will you need a culvert installed in a drainage ditch to gain access to the property, and if so how large?

Lot Size:

Is the property large enough to accommodate the size house you intend to build after the setbacks are taken into consideration?

Zoning and Restrictive Covenants:

Will setbacks and height restrictions have a negative effect on your ideas?

Are there any architectural restrictions that are not compatible with your intentions, that have been imposed by the municipality or the original land developer?

How about **deed restrictions?**

Here's a 'pit' you could easily fall into. **Deed restrictions** are not always a known factor and do not have a specific time limitation. A former owner could have restricted the use of the land to not more than one story of construction above grade a half century ago. And if you want to build a two story house you are in for some difficulties, economic, legal or both when some sharp researcher finds something that has been overlooked by less astute investigations into the title for the property. Deed restrictions can run in perpetuity. Virtually forever!

Utilities and Infrastructure:

What public utilities are in existence at the property now?

Are there special taxes or fees for sewer and water tap-ins?

Are there special assessments for school or highway construction?

What is the cost of a water meter in this municipality?

Will you need a well or septic system?

Will public sidewalks be required across the front of the property at your expense?

Are there any public utility or electric company easements on any part of the property? If so, will they in any way interfere with your idea?

You will also want to investigate taxes, availability of services such as trash pick-up, newspaper and mail delivery.

*Warning! Whenever somebody who is trying to sell you property, tells you that such and such a utility is close by, you had better check it out. 500 feet of 4" water line could cost you several thousand dollars to extend to the property. There could also be collateral expenses involved and considerable delay of your project.

Site Conditions:

You usually cannot tell if there are natural problems inherent to the property. For instance, how would you know if there was rock or muck three feet down? Unless there was outward evidence of rock outcropping, or marsh-like conditions apparent on the surface, you cannot tell just by looking.

Let's say the land you are looking at was filled a long time ago. There was a depressed swampy area right in the middle of it, the perfect spot to place a house. So a previous owner thought it would enhance the site to fill in this depression. Not deeply filled but just a foot or two, enough to obscure some unsightly features. The fill made the land nice and level and covered up what some former owner thought was a deterrent to salability.

There are some types or vegetation that will give you a clue. Other telltale signs, like evidence that water had been standing in a shallow depression in the middle of the land. You can see the outline of the dark rings left as the water receded into the ground. Color change and stunted growth of vegetation are also telltale signs.

Well, what have we here? Mulberry bushes growing around this depressed area. Mulberry bushes love marshy places. So do reed type growths, such as cat tails, rushes, succulents and tuberous plants. (CLUE) What caused the land to settle was the organic materials in the marsh being compressed by the weight of the fill and by deterioration of the organic materials themselves.

In order to build on this property now, all the fill and organic materials under it would have to be excavated and removed no matter how deep they go down! Then clean fill dirt would have to be placed into the excavation in 8" lifts (layers) and compacted mechanically to a density equal to 95%, before any constructions could take place there.

(After I promised not to get technical and then I dropped this one on you, so let me explain.) Density of 100% means the tightness of the earth molecules, if the earth had never been disturbed by any type of excavation.

What could prospective buyers do if they suspected a problem? I usually go to the building department that has jurisdiction in the area. They have knowledge of local conditions, and can often put you in touch with people who have first hand experience in these communities. I have on many occasions asked for and received permission to do test borings or spot excavations on properties that had great potential, but were suspect.

A very reliable source of information about property you may be interested in is the surveyors who have most recently done work on the property or who are active in that area. They often have first hand knowledge, even sometimes that property has been improperly filled.

Case History:

Deep Pit:
One day while visiting a real estate office I was invited to listen in on a conversation that was one of the most intriguing stories I have ever heard. This was about a muck problem on a woman's lot.

Carol V. had purchased a building lot in a rural area north of the city. She had hired a builder who obtained the permits and began construction. The footings for the foundation were dug, the reinforcing steel was in place and the builder called the county building department for the required footing inspection.

When the inspector arrived he immediately walked to the rear of the foundation and starred at a small pond toward the rear of the property. He seemed perplexed at what he saw and red tagged (rejection notice) the job, notifying the builder that the footings were dug into an unstable soil condition. The inspector had remembered this little pond as being somewhat larger when he had hunted in this area frequently a few years earlier.

It was determined that the pond had been partially filled in to make the lot saleable. The filled area occupied all the usable land up to the front setback line. The pond had taken up almost the entire lot at one time, and the lot was now worthless as a building site. The county condemmed the construction and the site!

Carol V. sued the people who sold her the property, who knew that the lot was a filled pond, and she lost the law suit! She was stuck with a worthless, un-saleable piece of property.

I met this lady several years after all this took place. I could not believe the court did not rule in her favor. I asked her where the property was and since it was in an area where I built frequently I assured her that I would inspect the condemned building site.

When I arrived, I saw one of the prettiest scenes you can imagine. It was a large deep lot, and the neighboring houses were setback a great distance from the road. A delightful pond occupied almost the rear third of the property, with a thicket of trees in the background. It was a picture perfect place to build a home.

I called Carol that evening with an idea that occurred to me. Would she invest $350. for some test borings and an opinion from my structural engineer? I explained what I had in mind. She agreed. If there was any hope of using the lot she was interested, so long as the cost was not beyond her means.

The test results revealed that the organic matter that was once the bottom of the pond and the fill that was dumped over it, went to a depth of 22 feet. Below that level there existed very stable soil conditions. My structural engineer confirmed that we could drive pilings 35 feet down, well into the stable soils. The pilings would easily support the weight of a large house.

Carol was elated. Plans and supporting data were submitted to the county. In a few weeks we had the required permits, and proceeded to build a beautiful Victorian house over the old condemned building site!

After living in the house for several years Carol married and moved away from the area. She sold her home and recovered all of her expenses plus a tidy profit. A very happy ending to what was once a bad dream.

The Bypassed Lots:

I have received a great deal of personal satisfaction many times over the years when I have purchased some unusual properties. They were the 'bypassed' lots, considered difficult to build on, undesirable and nearly impossible to sell even if something could be built there.

I do not recommend these tactics to the inexperienced, so don't get carried away and take a flyer on a 'cheap' lot. Cheap lots nearly always cost more in the final analysis. But armed with the knowledge that these properties offered a one of a kind opportunity for something unique, I could sometimes spot real winners among these unwanted. And I was able to bargain with the owners to boot. Some of them thought they had found a sucker, born just that moment!

Steep Terrain:

This is my strong forte. My first custom home subdivision in the late 50's was on top of the Ontario Escarpment in Western New York State. The area was solid limestone and looked like a giant terraced amphitheater, with a series of small cliffs descending down the face of a steep incline.

The cliffs were spaced almost uniformly at 250 foot intervals and allowed large lots to be developed with the roads on the flat parts between the cliffs. The building sites of several lots would be partly on the upper side of the cliffs, and partly on the lower portion. As Lake Ontario had receded over many millions of years, it had eroded the limestone into an ideal setting for **split site** ranch homes!

We refer to this type of building site as a **split site**, offering two levels of potential for some unusual home designs. My architect was ecstatic. He sketched up several ideas which I put on display in our model home and those lots along with houses sold out quickly. In fact the views were so spectacular from most locations in the subdivision, that we had record breaking sales.

The icing on the cake was that we outsold everybody in the building business, building non-basement houses in a strong traditional basement market. Many of our competitors predicted disaster when they heard we had purchased this acreage which had been on the market for many years.

There were other big pluses to this story. It taught me, early on in my education as a builder, that there is potential in properties that others consider almost worthless. And that imagination costs nothing. I love to build on steep terrain, and now you know why.

Ravine Construction:

Most people shy away from living in ravines and areas lower than the highways they front on. In most instances I agree that these situations are risky. But I have utilized some of these less desirable locations with houses designed to these sites, making them look like they grew there. In one instance the home was entered across a bridge over delightful sunken garden that was visible from the kitchen and several other parts of the house.

Land Sloping Down And Away From The Road:

This is another one of my favorite conditions. It offers a very unique opportunity for doing something surprising and useful. I use this condition to create a **walk-out** or **daylight basement**. The surprise is that from the street, the house appears to be one or two stories high, but actually contains another useful living level that can't be seen from the street side. Imagine a three story house, one level is actually below grade, and no worry about violating height limitations or restrictive covenants!

Corner Lots With Streets On Three Sides:

This is a very unusual occurrence and I have only been involved with such locations once. I was building in a beautiful community in Central Florida in the early 70's, and one day the developer asked me to look at the two lots flanking the entrance to Phase I of his prime subdivision. These two lots had been shunned by all prospects the sales force had worked with, and though sales were brisk, no prospect had ever expressed the slightest interest in these very prominent locations.

There were several disadvantages in addition to the streets on three sides. One of them was a major thoroughfare, with a good deal of traffic. The lots were flat and uninteresting, though one had several large pine trees. The other had almost no vegetation. The setbacks on corner lots were very restrictive, creating an unusually small rectangle of land available to accommodate a house. Was there a solution the developer asked?

A win, win situation was in the making for me. Phase II of the development was in progress directly across the busy avenue, with heavy earthmoving equipment in evidence. The were massive piles of dirt everywhere. It gave me a brainstorm.

I would buy both lots, I explained to the developer, and at a reduced price. But there were two other very important conditions that he would have to agree with, before I would make a final commitment. First, he would allow me unlimited fill dirt, (available directly across the road) to be placed by the earthmovers (pans) on both these lots, in whatever manner I wished.

Secondly, he would supply 6' high basket weave fencing along the property line fronting the busy highway for both lots and supply vine-like plantings along the earth bunker (sound baffle) I was going to create there. The fence (visual screen) was then to be built on top of the bunkers, (also called berms) as I specified. He readily agreed to all my conditions and we struck a deal.

I then contoured the lots to accept two specialty split site houses. One a front to rear split level, and the other, a two story, high level ranch house. Both these styles fit into the hillsides I had specially induced, to make all the newly created rolling terrain look as though it had always been there.

My competitors laughed so hard they couldn't stand up.

Not only did I beat them to the bank on this one, (both homes sold before completion) but both these unusual presentations induced several additional orders for reproductions on sloping land elsewhere. Everybody told me multi-level houses would never sell in Florida. I later was informed that these were the first multi-story homes built in that part of the state in over forty years!

I had the jump on my competitors, who were mistakenly convinced that multi-level houses were 'bombs' in Central Florida. Let me tell you friends, in six months they were all building multi-level houses. And I caught several of them sneaking around my projects with cameras and tape measures to see how it was done. Ho! Ho! Ho!

There is one very important idea that I wish to advance to you in all these tales. The objective in blending house and building site is to utilize the property to the '**highest and best use**'. This is a rule you should always keep foremost in your thoughts, when considering a land purchase for any purpose and what you intend to do with it. How to use it to best advantage!

Drainage And Erosion Control:

This is a vast subject. There are countless conditions we could discuss, that would fill several volumes. Of course you will grade your land so that surface water runs away from your house. An important consideration is what happens to the runoff water once it leaves your property. You can't just dump it anywhere. The building department and banks will insist on a good drainage plan. You should seek professional help in this area, especially if you have unusual or difficult circumstances to deal with.

Erosion can be a serious problem particularly on steep inclines. Design professionals can assist you in overcoming this potential hazard.

'**Slow the flow**'. That's an easy rule to remember. You can probably figure most of it out yourself. "Water flow down hill. Steep hill make water run fast. Make big mess. Must make water move slow." No! An Indian Chief did not teach me that.

Control Measures:

Several come to mind. Terracing (steps), trenching, culverts, catch basins, swails, rip rap, storm water diverters, reservoirs, to name a few. Many of these techniques and contrivances can be made to enhance the appearance of your property. In one subdivision where I was building, a 6' wide drainage (ditch) easement ran along the boundaries of several lots, all of which were being bypassed by our prospects until we lined the sides of the ditch with rocks (rip-rap). They sold out the next weekend. Get knowledgeable people to assist you with this important part of your planning.

9

Solar Orientation:

When you are standing there for the first time, gazing out at the distant view, the sun giving forth all its radiance, a refreshing breeze caressing your face, and your brain is screaming, "This is it baby!", you know for sure you have found your dream place. That's probably the way you want your house to face too, the way that enticed you into buying this land in the first place. Prevailing winds and how the sun rises and sets over your property should be a factor in your planning.

Perimeter Survey:

This is a drawing or a map of the property boundaries. It is a verification of all significant information related to the distances between the corners of your property, and other relevant data.

Topographical Survey:

This survey describes the surface features of a property. It consists of a series of contour lines that indicate changes in elevation, the lines being spaced in particular increments. i.e. each line will indicate a distance of 5' of incline. This data is frequently included on perimeter surveys, if requested.

In Conclusion:

Site selection and site planning are really not such a hard job after all. Right? Did I mention that I think flat lots are okay too? I have seen a great deal of advertising proclaiming the wonders of level land for building sites. I have built on thousands of them. Everybody doesn't want to live on a hill.

Seaside, lakefront, sites on rivers, ponds and creeks are all wonderful locations, many of which will require special types of construction if they are located in **flood zones**. This subject will be covered in a later part of this book.

PART 2
Planning the Project:

Getting Started:

Some ancient Chinese sage put it thus: "A journey of a thousand miles begins with a single step". So the logical thing to do is to take that first step. If you have come this far, then an idea has begun to take shape in your mind. You have thought about it for such a long time that you know exactly what you want. Now it's time to make your dream into a reality. A realistic budget should be established as one of your initial steps. No point in starting out planning something beyond your means, or at variance with your objectives.

Choosing the Plan:

For some this will be a simple step. They may have already run across an idea in a shelter magazine, or seen a house they like, and they want to do something similar. Try to formulate a plan into a realistic idea. Sketch it on paper, or gather some pictures of ideas you like, things you want to incorporate into your plans.

But let me give you a word of warning about this stage. It is here, in the early formulation of your idea that you need to begin practicing self-discipline. If you get carried away at this point you may be in for many disappointments, a rather unhappy beginning. Plan the work and then work the plan. It is much easier to make a small house bigger than to make a big house smaller.

Choosing a Designer:

There are several important aspects in choosing a good designer. The way many people find the right person is through word of mouth and reputation. If she/he has construction experience, that is a big plus. Most designers have never built and do not have first hand experience in knowing how things actually go together in the field applications.

There are well-known local architects or draftsmen who have good track records in your community. Many examples of their work already exist. Interview one or two whose work you like. Have her/him show you sample plans and explain to you what they will include in the working drawings.

Ask them to outline the scope of the work they will perform on the plans and in other services, like helping you write the outline specifications. Many designers are also aware of all the necessary information needed to satisfy the requirements of the building departments and banks. Ask what the fees will be for your plans, etc.

Cost Effective Design:

A very important part of your conversation must be **cost effective design**. Creating cost effective working drawings is not just drawing lines on paper. It is one of the most important ways to save you money. It begins with sizing the construction to best accommodate **modular components**. Building materials are made mostly in standard sizes like 4'x8' for plywood and other laminates. That's modular. Standard sized.

The concrete block and framing lumber are also produced in modular sizes. It simply works out to mean 'even numbers' for dimension lumber. Like 2x4's. They are available in 8', 10', 12', 14', 16', lengths and so on. If you build 9' high wood frame walls you will have to use 10' 2x4's and there will be at least a foot of waste from each one that has to be cut to size.

Concrete block is made in many sizes, all modular, but the most commonly used in residential construction is 8"x 8"x16". If you stack them on top of each other (courses) two will equal 16", three will be 24", and so on, all totals being modular numbers.

Three standard concrete blocks laid end to end will equal 4 feet of length. So we keep running across these same numbers over and over again. Four feet is divisible by 8", 12", 16", 24", and 32" and 48". These numbers are repetitious in most building materials made is the U.S.A. If you needed floor joists 15 feet long you would have to buy 16 footers.

Neither you nor your designer should loose sight of the modular factor throughout the designing stages of your plan. This is where a good designer can help pay for part of her/his fee in cost saving to you.

Example of a foundation size:

Which would be more economical in terms of modular? 24'x44' or 23'x45'?

Get the picture? How about this one? You would like a great room in your house with 9'-6" high walls. You saw it done in a model home and you really have your heart set on it. But for almost no difference in cost, you can have ten foot high walls. They both require the same amount of lumber and drywall (waste factors considered).

I am not stating that you should never deviate from modular sizes, but try to utilize them wherever possible and practical to your idea. The old adage "Waste not want not", comes to mind, because that is what cost effectiveness is all about.

The Outline Specification:

I earlier mentioned an **outline specification**, and if your designer is going to prepare this document for you, it essential that you describe any particular materials you want to use. If you are leaving it up to the designer, make sure to give instructions to not be lavish in making these decisions. Specifying materials or methodology, with which you are not familiar, could be costly and confusing to you.

Construction Documents:

As a general practice your contractor will supply the outline specification as part of the **construction documents** package. But if you or your architect is putting the project out for bid, then generating the construction documents will be your/his responsibility.

This may sound like some complex set of papers but basically they amount to construction drawings, site plan, specifications, contract(s) and incidental things pertaining to the construction process, i.e. inclusions expressed in the contract that require all or part of another documents to be included (such as the **construction draw schedule**.)

Construction Draw Schedule:

This is a schedule outlining when monies are paid to the contractor/builder. It specifies what work processes and materials placements must be completed before payment can be made.

Writing the Specs:

Have your designer make general suggestions if you have not decided on exactly how to handle the specs. If you are going to take bids then be sure to instruct whoever writes the specs to include the most essential elements from your own outline. This way all bids the will be based on the exact same information being given to each bidder, so hopefully there will be no misinterpretations.

An Outline Specification:

Is a detailed list of materials, products, and methodology that will be used in your project. You can supply your designer with a list of things you are definitely going to want. But you should be aware that bigger is not always better in selecting sizes of structural components. Bigger can cost many more dollars than a smaller size that will do the job adequately.

An example of this is when sizing floor joists. The **'clear span'** is the longest distance between the supports that the ends of the joists will rest on. Building codes, architectural, and engineering manuals and many structural component manufacturers publications, contain span tables to help in selecting sizes of framing members according to the wood species being used.

Some species are harder, have greater strengths and are more desirable for particular applications. If a hem/fir 2x8 will suffice, why spend your money on Douglas fir 2x12's?

And I want to point out that the span tables contain safety factors that recommend more than minimum requirements for each wood species commonly in use. In effect, hem/fir 2x8's spaced on 16" centers, on a 'clear span' of 10 feet are totally acceptable.

Let me back up just a little here to insure that my explanation is clear to you. The **'clear span'** is the longest distance between the points where the floor joist will rest; in other words bearing points (block walls, wood frame partitions, beams etc).

The reference to 16" centers is a reference to the distance from the middle of one framing member to the middle of the next at either side. This '**spacing**' is uniformly 16" c/c (center to center) or expressed as 16" o/c (on center) which you will see on your working drawings.

Spacing for other structural elements may vary but will most often be spaced at 16", 24" and in rare instances 32", in residential work. Some types of construction will specify much greater spacing between framing members.

Grade Stamps and Other Markings:

Let me insert here a brief explanation of some of the common terminology used in expressing grades and species of lumber, since you will see these markings on each piece of wood that comes to your job site. I will explain some other common markings you will see occasionally as well. Now when you see them you will know what they mean.

Construction Grade:
Mark:= *construction or const.* 2x's that will be used in structural applications.

Stud Grade:
Mark:= *stud.* 2x4's commonly used in frame walls

Standard:
Mark:= *standard or stand.* 2x4's used in non-structural applications

Utility:
Mark:= *util.* 2x4's frequently mixed with standard, in non-structural applications

No. 1 and No. 2 Stress grades:

Used in the manufacture of structural components, roof and floor trusses because of strength characteristics. Since these components consist of many pieces you may have to look around to find a grade stamp.

Common Pit:

What is nominal dimension?

I will introduce you to a phrase you may not have ever heard or with which you may not be familiar. I do not intend to insult your intelligence so if you know about this just play along and let me explain it to the less fortunate. I have met framing carpenters who, while totally aware of what the term means, were not familiar with this particular terminology. So, after that long winded speech let me elaborate.

When we talk about 2x4's we are talking **nominal dimension**. This piece of wood is 2" thick and 4" wide *in name only*. If you were to measure one, without knowing about this 'clever deception' you would find that the so called 2"x4" stud (board) was actually only 1-1/2" thick and 3-1/2" wide!

"Why those dirty low down………………"

Before you get too excited I will give you some more information. Lumber and plywood standards and grading rules for lumber have been established by the forestry industry and the U.S. Government. A 2x4 starts out as a rough-sawn piece of wood that does measure 2 inches by 4 inches. It is then 'sized' to the smooth format that you buy in the lumberyard or home improvement store.

All dimension lumber goes through the same process. You pay the price for the rough sawn board footage, as it is cut from the logs, before the lumber is 'sized' or 'dressed', i.e. 2x6 = 1-1/2" x 5-1/2", 2x8 = 1-1/2" x 7-1/2", and so on. However, as the width of the lumber size increases you may find an additional variance. A 2x10 may measure only 9-1/4" and a 2x12, 11-3/16" sometimes even less. You will find these variations to be quite common. Just roll with the punches friends.

Board Foot:

And now that I have introduced the term '**board foot**' I will introduce you to a simple method to calculate the board footage in any given piece of dimension lumber. Simple multiplication and division. Short quiz: How many board feet of lumber are there in one 2x4 that is 10 feet long? Here's how simple it is.

The equation is expressed: $\dfrac{2 \times 4}{12}$

A piece of wood 12"x 12"x1" thick = 1 **board foot**.

Solution: 2x4=8, 8 divided by 12 = .67 or 2/3 of a **board foot**.

So then we multiply .67 by 10 feet and come up with 6.7 or 6-2/3 BM which (bm = board measure) is the symbol for board feet. Now isn't that slick? When those hot shots talk board feet around you they will not be able to pull the board foot over your eyes!

Case History:
Many years ago I was building a house for a financial wizard. He was one of those work-a-holic types and I rarely ever saw him, but his wife came to look at the progress of the work almost every day. We were in the process of framing the first floor walls and soon after we started this phase of the work, I received an urgent call from a person whom I had never met.

He began the telephone conversation by introducing himself as the attorney for my whiz kid client. The first words out of his mouth were something to the effect that we had to tear down all the wood framing that had taken place because the lumber being used was sub-standard and under sized. "Why the two by fours are only 3-1/2 inches wide!", he exclaimed. "The lumber you are using is a complete fraud!"

Then he demanded that I be in his office at exactly 4 P.M. that afternoon to review the specifications with he and his/my client, the whiz kid.

This was my reply: "Mr. so and so, my fee for that kind of instruction is $150. per hour with a four hour minimum. If you have any doubts about the authenticity of the wood products I am using and their sizing on that job, then I suggest you contact the local Lumberman's Association and get your education from them!"

I never heard anything further on the subject, from either the mouthpiece or my client. In fact they were very timid for the remainder of the project.

There are new products in the marketplace, which are worth mentioning. Many of them have to do with the technology of **wood fiber engineering**.

They are structural components and for the most part epoxy laminates, made from strands of wood fibers. The wood fiber is removed from logs, and reconfigured into composite timbers that are four times the strength of a solid wood timber of the same size.

One such product is marketed under the name Parallam*™ which I had the distinction of introducing into the Florida Residential Market for the manufacturer, Truss-Joist MacMillan Corporation, in 1992. This same company also manufactures Truss-Joists, which can be substituted for dimension lumber (2x8, 2x10, and 2x12) when greater strengths and longer spans are desirable.

I like all the products made by this company. They are well engineered, and competitively priced, and have simplified countless structural applications for me over the years. In fact they will help you or your designer with your structural design if you are going to use their products.

I have been paid nothing for mentioning TJM in this book.

Common Wood Species and Symbols:

Common Wood species used in residential work:

DF= Douglas fir
SYP= southern yellow pine
Hem= hemlock. HF hem/fir
SP= spruce
LP= Lodgepole pine
Cedar= cedar cdr
S-Dry= sawn dry
S-Gr.= sawn green
K-D= kiln dried
PAD= partly air-dried.

Moisture Content:

This very important factor is not indicated by any markings you will see on the dimension lumber you may purchase for your project. It can change depending on how it has been stored, exposure to the elements and atmospheric conditions. Framing lumber should contain not over 20% **moisture content** preferably less. A moisture meter is used to determine the amount of moisture in any given piece of lumber or log. Kiln dried framing lumber will usually contains about 19% **moisture content.**

There are frequently mill numbers on lumber, and even shift numbers on plywood and other laminated products that are likely to be used on your project. I always make a note of the manufacturer's name, the mill number and the shift, which is stamped on plywood. That does not mean I examine every sheet for stamps, but I look to see if most of them have the same marks and keep track of this information for a very important reason.

If there is any de-lamination, or failure of the glue system, I launch a 'protest' through the supplier from whom I purchased the plywood. This means a representative of the manufacturer must come to inspect the defect and make adjustment(s) in terms of material and labor costs, to remove and replace the defective material.

I have never lost a 'protest', although one manufacturer refused to make good for the labor of an undeniable failure of their product after it was already in place.

The supplier made good for the labor, but I began a boycott of that manufacturer's products ever since then and they have lost several million dollars of business over the past twenty years as a result.

After I have dragged you through all this dry stuff you deserve a break. I will now tell you a funny story that my architect used to spring on people wherever the conversation at social gatherings where he was present, swung to construction. He always began this tale as though it was a true story.

Two guys drove an old truck up to a local lumberyard one day and one of them went inside to make an inquiry. He walked up to the counter where one of the sales clerks greeted him. "Good afternoon sir! How may I help you?"

The man replied, "You got any 4x2's?"

"You mean 2x4's, sir. Yes, we have them. How many do you want?"

The man slapped himself on the forehead and blurted out, "Geez, I doan know, I'll hafta go out to da truck an ax my brudder." Whereupon he went back out to the truck. A lengthy conversation ensued and the man came back into the office. "We want 350 of 'em."

"Okay," said the clerk. "How long do you want them?"

The man again slapped himself on the forehead and stated, "Geez, I doan know! I'll hafta go out in da truck and ax my brudder."

Another long conversation followed out in the truck and the man finally came back into the yard office. "We're gonna want 'em for a long time. We're gonna build a house wid 'em!"

Well, I thought it was funny. After all, how many humorous things can you say about a 4x2,…..er 2x4?

Let me say it once more. ***Cost effectiveness begins on the drawing board.***

If you get it right there, you are off to a strong start. Remember also, that you do not have to build a fortress. The building codes are in place to insure that your project is in conformance with sound building practice.

There are many safety valves built into the codes for your protection. So unless it is something that you are adamant about, don't spend your money on over design unless it makes you feel good and you have bucks to spare.

The Ten Most Important Things You Want In Your New Home:

Make a list for yourself. Think it over carefully and describe every item.

Then make another list of the next ten most important things you want in your new home. Now study those lists in detail. Go back and put a little check mark on the items you are willing to compromise.

I have a favorite comment about these lists. **"You can't get five pounds (of stuff) into a four pound bag".** Go back check off some more of your twenty 'most important things that you just cannot live without in your new home list'. You can't get it all under one roof. Well, maybe you can, if you have unlimited time and resources.

When prospective clients describe their sometimes complex projects to me and ask, "Can you do that?", my answer is, "If you give me enough time and enough money I can build anything."

Be Objective and Realistic:

Things can be very trying at this juncture. Something's gotta give! But don't ever let it get emotional. Probably the most common root of unhappiness is disappointment. That's something we live with all of our lives, and getting emotional over building a house is self defeating.

Something doesn't go your way and then everything else falls apart. Then another emotional free fall. But the reality is that you would probably have to eliminate some of your 'musts' once you start getting price quotes. So get real, right from the beginning.

Embarrassing Pit:

I had a very amusing experience with the wife of a client not too long ago. Here's what happened. We had just poured some concrete columns, which were part of the foundation of a large beach house I was building for the lady and her husband.

These structures were in a place that until that time was very large and open, only because the work had not progressed to the point where the columns were necessary. But suddenly, "her beautiful open space" was a cluttered mess of form work and bracing. The lady was totally devastated! She forthwith announced that she hated the house, and was never going to move into it, nor was she even going to look at it again.

Her husband was at a complete loss to explain this sudden turn of events. A large laundry facility, a shop, and quarters for live-in help would occupy this part of the house on the ground level. The lady of the house was lamenting to any willing ear, and it was soon common knowledge that some catastrophe had befallen the project causing the poor woman no end of distress. She absolutely hated the house, and was in an extremely emotional state.

She never spoke any of her vehemence to me directly but curious neighbors were asking what happened. I had only head the news second hand, but when I met her face to face a few days later she was once again happy and content, but somewhat red-faced. It seems the dear lady thought we were building the columns in her great room, which happened to be located one floor above. One of life's embarrassing moments.

What Should the Working Drawings Contain?

The basics are quite simple. Residential drawings should consist of, as a minimum, the following:

Site Plan Drawing:

Every building department and bank will require this sheet. It is a picture of how your improvements will be located on your property, distances from lot lines, etc. Some building departments will have a detailed list of requirements, which must be included on your site plan.

The site plan drawing will resemble an enlarged version of your perimeter survey with much or all of the data contained on that survey, including topographical information and information showing how you intend to handle the drainage. Your building department will give you an outline containing any special requirements.

Foundation Plan:

Whether **basement**, or **monolithic slab**, **stem wall** or **crawl space**, this sheet must show the particulars of all structural elements inherent to the foundation, including steel re-enforcing applications.

Floor Plan(s):

Everybody knows this one. After all it is probably the most thought out, talked about aspect of the entire planning process. It will show how the spaces in your house will be separated, door and window locations, sometimes electrical, and heating/air conditioning layouts, and should include cross sections of detailing necessary to instruct those who work the plan.

Cross Section:

Some building departments require a full section drawing (cut away through the entire house.) Door and window jamb details and structural details are often included as well as room finish schedules depending on available space on the pages.

Elevations:

This is a drawing of the exterior views of the building so you can see what it looks like form outside. Though it does not necessarily have anything to do with actual elevation above sea level, you may find references as to height of the entire building above existing grade on these sheets.

This is potentially a picture of what your house will look like. WHAT YOUR HOUSE IS GOING TO LOOK LIKE SHOULD BE OF EXTREME IMPORTANCE TO YOU! Here is where style, color and texture come into play. No! You will not be selecting actual color at this point, but you know what colors you like.

Also being aware of how texture can enhance the looks of your home. Sidings, exterior trim, horizontal and vertical lines can be used to emphasize important architectural elements that you want to be most noticed.

Examples: the use of brick, stone, stucco, rough sawn wood, smooth wood, vinyl, bric-a-brac, to name a few.

Fenestration:

Oh! Oh! After promising to keep it simple here comes the heavy stuff. Well, relax. This is a big word that means, arranging the windows in the exterior walls. See? I had you worried. But as simple as this process may sound, it can probably be one of the most important design elements responsible for how good your house will look standing out there on that wonderful location it took so long for you to find.

Fenestration is an important factor in creating good style for your home, because windows project, or suggest a particular kind of character for your house.

Special Note: Remember to consider what is happening to the exterior appearance of your home whenever you are working with window and exterior doors locations while arranging inside wall space. Make sure what you are doing inside is not having an adverse effect on the exterior style. I give precedence to the exterior whenever I have to choose small convenience on the inside over style for the outside.

Windows have their own style. Colonial is a window style. How so? This means the window is divided into many little panes (pains when you're washing them) or **lites,** which is industry jargon. Traditionally, 'Early American' (colonial) windows had many **lites** because the technology of glass making way back then was not advanced enough to produce affordable, durable glass in large thin sheets.

If you are building an 'Early American' style house, or prefer that look, then the traditional divided lites colonial windows would be a natural choice. Victorian is another style window that utilizes the glass divisions to create a distinctive and unique character all its own.

Contemporary can mean anything. It is oftentimes a state of mind, but contemporary windows can be undivided large panes, geometric shapes, and freeform.

Common Pit:

Have you ever seen an ugly house? Would you want to live in one? Do not let your home be ugly. Don't let anybody tell you it doesn't matter, because that is silly. Even if it is small it's not going to be invisible. Style it to the very best advantage. Remember this; someday this house may be on the market. You will want it to have every advantage you can muster at that time, and good style will be an important factor.

My architect spends a good deal of time on styling my products, not only the front, but the back and sides as well. He knows that not only do I want '**curb appeal**' but '**back yard appeal**' also. When I build those three story walkout basement houses my architect takes special care to create the best looking three-story houses known to mankind. Resale! Resale! Resale!

Floor Framing Plan:

This/these sheet(s) will show the details of how the joists (framing members) of the floor will be placed, spaced and fastened. It will indicate the sub-floor materials, bridging/blocking and fastenings, and any structural details pertinent to the floor wafer structure, including all intermediate bearing structures on which the floor joists rest. Required by most building departments.

Roof Framing Plan:

This/these sheet(s) will show the size(s) and spacing of rafters, the ridge beam(s), describe the size and location of any roof openings (skylights) dormers, cupolas or other appurtenant roof structures and roof sheathing; will describe the finish roofing materials and **underlaments**. It will usually show details of **flashing** and other waterproofing devices at roof opening, roof intersections, and special installations pertinent to the roof.

The following are required by most building departments.

Plumbing and Schematics:

A few building departments will require these drawings for single family residential work, but I have rarely run into them over the years. If you do need them in your drawings they will show how the piping would look if you drew it like a tree from top to bottom, with pipe sizing, vents, water lines and waste piping. Some want information related to water conservation, i.e. gallons per flush of water closets (johns).

HVAC: Heating Ventilating Air Conditioning:

On rare occasions I have known building departments to require separate drawing for these installations in single family residential work. However, you will almost invariably be required to provide energy calculations, which can be usually be provided by your designer or HVAC contractor.

WARNING PIT:

Working drawings are required to be in scale, most common being ¼" = 1 foot. Some details or section drawings may be done in larger scale for clarity, or in smaller scale to conserve space. If for any reason you must use some other scale on residential drawings, *especially floor plans,* you should make sure there are many **LARGE BOLD** indications all over the plan pages that are affected, otherwise you will have a disaster on your hands.

People in the construction industry are creatures of habit, and having drawings in quarter inch scale is a long time habit for most of them! **A BIG ONE! Don't let a designer talk you into some uncommon scale just because she/he wants to save paper.**

Financing the Project:

If you will be applying for a mortgage to finance construction, you will need to supply your banker with all the exhibits we have outlined in the foregoing. It is good business to submit the most comprehensive working drawings and specifications to your bank because good detailing on these documents are favorably received by the appraisers. You want a good appraisal.

I think one of the most often repeated remarks I have heard over the years is; "I wish I had known about that before I built!" And I am astounded at how a little simple information, in advance, could have helped someone avoid a pitfall or two. Just being fore-armed with a little knowledge could have a great impact on how you will fare in your attempts to get your dreams made into reality.

Avoiding mistakes and making good decisions is the name of the game. None of us is perfect, so if you make a couple of little booboos along the way, it's no biggie. Just never loose your cool, and keep moving ahead!

The "I Wish I Had Known About That Before I Built" List.

Now that we have the preliminaries out of the way, I will tell you about this list. This book is *that list.* This book is what I want you to know about. If you use the information provided in these pages, you have a detailed outline of what it takes to build a new home, with a minimum of surprises. Complicated? Sure it is! But are you afraid? Going to change your mind now? Nah! Let's move on.

PART 3
Putting Your Plan Out For Bids

Now that you have worked so hard and finalized your plans and specs you are ready for the bid or **negotiating process**.

Inviting Bidders:

There are many methods for getting contractors to bid on your plans. You can advertise for bids in construction industry publications especially in existence for that purpose. Those invited by your architect will then come in to his office to pick up the construction documents and instructions to bidders. I won't go into the details of this process, as it is not designed for residential work unless it is a very large job.

Taking bids through your designer is another method. They usually know reliable builders of good reputation and can save much time by inviting two or three of them to give you a firm price. You may want to include builders whose work you are familiar with, and who are already known to you.

I would suggest getting two or three builders interested, rather than using an industry publication to attract bidders. I have never bid on residential work. Most people come to me as a result of being familiar with my track record, and some of my specific projects. 99% of my business comes from referrals.

The Bid Package:

The essentials of a bid package are working drawings, specifications, a description of any alternate addendum you want to consider, and instructions to the bidders. All bidders must receive identical packages in order for you to get true competitive and realistic pricing. You may also solicit opinions on cost savings ideas from the bidders with alternate pricing for their suggestions.

Receiving and Opening the Bids:

When bidding commercial work contractors are required to submit their bid in sealed envelopes, which are presented to the architect. Then, with all bidders present, the bids are opened and read aloud. The low bid usually gets the project. This is the fair and honest way of taking bids. This method is rarely used in single family residential construction, mainly because the process is time consuming and involves additional costs for all parties. Don't waste your money. It would only be an ego trip.

The Negative Side of Taking Bids:

I will now outline my thoughts on the bid process. It's fine for commercial and industrial work. It *never fails* to induce *higher prices* from residential bidders.

The word 'bid' in itself will cause the flags to go up for most residential builders, because they most often get their business through different circumstances. The good builders are usually busy and that leaves the not so good ones looking for business who may take a flyer on a bid. So which will it be for you?

I'm going to let you in on a big secret, a real banger. The sure way to the best deal getting you project built is not by taking bids! I'm going to show you how you can make it happen and why it will. Just read on.

The Negotiated Price:

Have you ever gone out shopping for something you were sure you would find easily and then spend a great deal more time locating it that you ever expected? Frustrating! And a big waste of time. You found just what you wanted in your last stop. You knew you would find it there when you started out because that store has everything, but sometimes tends to be a little pricey. Just that you wanted to shop around a little to satisfy your curiosity.

Let's use a similar scenario to find a couple of builders to talk with about your building plans. You have already toured several model homes of one, and have inspected two houses that another builder had under construction. You have satisfied your urge to shop around. You are impressed with both but one seems to have flair, somewhat more imagination than the other.

You call both and make appointments to discuss your building program. They both agree to review your plans and give you an idea of costs and make cost saving suggestions. You have reached the stage of negotiating the price. But there is a big decision to be made here and you want to make the right choice. ***Selecting your builder*** Wow! This is a biggie!

Construction Management:

The Ultimate Negotiated Contract

Construction Management is a concept that I personally have employed for many types of construction. It is a departure from the traditional adversarial relationship created by conventional contracts between contractor and client, and replaces it by the formation of a team. This new 'team' relationship brings the contractor 'in house', becoming the construction liaison for the client. They are on the same side!

Basically, the contractor and the client agree to work together. The contractor's responsibilities do not change, but he now makes the client privy to all costs, and other sensitive data, normally held in strict confidence. The arrangement stipulates a fixed fee for the contractor, who agrees to accept a lesser profit for the advantage of not having to bid the job. The client has the benefit of the reduced costs and both benefit by working together rather than at arm's length. This arrangement has been very cost effective for many of my recent clients.

For many people the 'Getting Started' sequence will begin here.
You will discover how as you read on.

Selecting Your Builder:

You have already covered some ground of making your selection because you have done some important legwork. In the process of narrowing down your choices you should have accomplished a good portion of checking out the person you will ultimately choose to build your dream home. I will outline the most essential steps even though they my be repetitious.

Pierre Renaldo

A Check up list:

Look at samples of the builder's work:
You can get a good feel for the quality of the products. Compare that with other work you have seen.

Ask for Personal References:
And then check them out. You should try to talk to at least three past clients.

Ask for Credit References:
Good credit standing is a reflection of good business sense, and sound business practice.

Check the Credentials:
Is licensing is required? What about Workmen's Compensation, and liability insurance.

Check with your bank:
Banks know the reliable builders and their reputations.

Talk to the building department where your house is going to be built: This is a good source of information about builders.

What Should You Look For In A Builder?

Good Reputation:
This is probably how you will first hear about builders, by reputation. Their reputation is made up of many factors. Reliability, honesty, temperament, credibility, knowledge, talent, imagination, experience, trustworthiness, diligence, persistence, and personality.

Do you have good vibes about this person? You know when you like or don't like somebody, sometimes almost as soon as you have met. Do you like this particular individual?

Do not do business with anyone in whom you do not have feelings of trustworthiness. Mutual trust is essential in any good business relationship. Remember that you have to instill the same kind of confidences in your builder about yourself. We will cover some very important do's and don'ts on this subject later.

Does a depth of knowledge emanate when this person explains things? Do you understand this person easily? Are the answers direct and conclusive?

Are you enlightened when your questions are answered?

Obvious Track Record:

When you travel around looking at many builders' products, and you keep seeing the same builder's signs, then it will become obvious to you that this builder is popular. You can recognize the work of some builders even if their signs are not on a property, because they have unique style.

Unique Style:

It is almost like handwriting or better yet a signature. Their homes stand out wherever they are built. If you are noticing, then you already have good feelings about someone you don't even know, because you like the way these houses look. The builder has style, and is style conscious. Very good sign!

I built many Victorian homes while I was in business in Florida. People would tell me they recognized my 'signature' on all of them, because they were true Old Florida type homes.

They Are Always Evident:

Good builders advertise. They contribute to the communities where they build. They 'give some back', and leave a legacy of good form behind. You become familiar with the name(s). They are always 'around'.

They are not necessarily the big builders, but they are the prominent builders. They are the ones who truly make a difference. Deal with people who care about their clients. You can tell by their finished products, and their past clientele.

Here is an important aside that may be of help to some of you. You can start off by going to the builder of your choice before you get involved in any of the foregoing. Builders often offer plans and specs from their own catalog of homes. If this approach interests you, then you may find a plan and price you like in this manner. In that event you can avoid all the steps outlined in Part 2 of this book.

Isn't this all becoming a cakewalk?

PART 4
The First Giant Step

The Permitting Process:

The actual procedures of applying for permits may vary from place to place, but in essence they are similar to what I am about to describe. This is the providence of your builder.

Applying for the permit(s):

The building department of jurisdiction for your project will require some exhibits to be submitted along with the application for permit(s). Site plans, working drawings, a copy of your survey, and a variety of paperwork that such bureaucracies seem to thrive on. Your builder will gather up all this information on your behalf and get it submitted.

Plan Review:

Your esteemed building department will then review the plans to insure they conform to current building codes, zoning, restrictive covenants if any, and any other regulations that may apply. Then, after a prolonged interval, they are ready to issue the permit(s). Some highway departments get into the act at this point because they are the people who (in some instances) issue driveway permits. And the fire marshal has to have his say too.

Once all these guys have had their shot, the permit is ready to be issued.

The fee for the construction will be based on the amount of the square footage, cubic footage, number of rooms, toilets, light fixtures, and number of stories or whatever. Then you will be given the sad news.

If you are going to build in a resort or one of the major growth areas, like Florida you may be faced with the following types of charges built into the cost of your permit(s): Check these factors while you are in the process of acquiring your property and you will have planned on these additional costs.

Impact Fees:

This is a form of taxation imposed on new construction because it makes an impact on the community; infrastructures, schools, police and fire protection, water, sewage, etc. Let me assure you that the list keeps growing, as do the fees. In some places in Florida, impact fees will add as much as ten to twenty thousand dollars to the cost of your home. That's a lot of money for the privilege of living in a particular county, town or city.

Water and Sewer Tap in Fees:

These are special fees for districts that have expanded or revamped infrastructure and require these special assessments in order to recover costs.

Driveway and Curb Cut Fees:

In communities that have curbs along the roadways, you may have to pay for cutting through the curb, and repairing it when you install your driveway.

Water Meter Fee:

Most communities charge for water meters.

Utility Bonds:

In some locals, a bond is required to insure against damage to public utilities that front or cross your property in some manner. There are free underground locator services that will mark the locations of pipes and cables adjacent to your job site, so these utilities are not disturbed by necessary excavations on your property.

Variance Fees:

Should you apply for any form of variance to zoning regulations because of special requirements for your project, there is usually an application fee for this process. Variances should be sought long before you go to the permitting process. Avoid variances like the plague.

Case History Pit:

Several years ago I was the winning bidder on a large addition the county intended to build onto a branch library that was located on a barrier island off the coast of Florida. The application for permits was rejected because the flood zone elevation requirements for the first floor of the addition were obligatory to be seven feet higher than the existing building. The county was not able to circumvent this FEMA requirement, to grant itself a height variance and the project was cancelled. The county neglected to check this very critical factor before they wasted the taxpayer's money on drawings. See! Even the big boys make mistakes!

More details about flood zones will be covered later in this book.

Pierre Renaldo

PART 5
Beginning the Work Process

I will now walk you through the steps of actually getting the building under way. Each event will be listed in the sequence in which it would ordinarily occur. There may be some variations due to climatic conditions or local custom, but this is generally how things happen.

Site Preparation:

Building permit is posted prominently at front of the site. Port-a-John on premises for workers. All lot corners are located and flagged. We can't go bulldozing our neighbor's property by accident. All organic matter and topsoil is removed from the building site and stored in an out of the way place on the property.

The property is rough graded to provide level ground at the site, temporary drainage away from the building location and to allow ease of movement for workers, vehicles and materials. The house is 'staked out' in accordance with the site plan. You will see batter boards placed on the periphery of the site. These temporary 'fences' are used to locate the foundation, its height and all pertinent information for excavation and concrete/block/foundation placement.

It is important to note that provisions for temporary water, electricity and sanitation are provided at the site. Access for construction vehicles should also be completed. It is ideal to have the foundation accessible from all sides for ease of material deliveries and concrete trucks.

Excavation:

Whether you are digging a basement, footings, or preparing the forms for monolithic slab, this is an exacting process. Before any concrete is poured, all dimensions of the foundation should be double-checked. Likewise with the setbacks, to insure the building is properly located. Depth and location of sanitary sewer, storm sewer, if any, water lines, gas mains, telephone cables etc. should be determined in advance of any excavation.

Water, sewer and underground trenches for electric and gas utilities are often excavated at this time, especially if deep (basement) excavations are required. Precautions should be taken to place barricades and/or colored ribbon in highly visible locations around excavated areas for safety purposes.

The Foundation:

Before we move into this topic let me talk to you about concrete and some of its characteristics. This is one of the most common parts of almost any construction project and discussions about it can become very technical.

You may see some things on the foundation plan or the specs that you are not sure about. I will start with concrete strengths. You could run across this number; *3000 psi*. This is the **test strength** of the concrete specified. Certain proportions of the ingredients used in the mixing of concrete will produce this **test strength**. It is not likely that there will be a weight of 3000 pounds per square inch exerted any place in the foundation of your house.

The number is derived from a test conducted on a cylinder of concrete 6" in diameter and 12" high. When an architect or engineer on a big construction project orders this test to be conducted, it involves several of these cylinders which are filled with the concrete being poured in some phase of that particular project.

Some cylinders are left at the construction site, and others are taken to a laboratory where the concrete test is to take place. Concrete gains strength as it ages. Usually it will reach the designated test strength in about 30 days or less, but tests are conducted on some of cylinders at earlier intervals.

Here's what happens. The concrete is removed from the metal cylinder and placed in a machine that will exert enough weight on the concrete to cause it to break. The pounds per square inch or psi number is derived from the amount of weight that causes that failure. If the machine registers 3,280 psi when the concrete is 30 days old, then it had attained at least the **test strength** specified.

The reason that some cylinders are broken at earlier intervals is to catch problems early, especially in heavy construction. A test conducted in three days may result in a 2,000-pound break. That would indicate that the concrete was curing very quickly. Then another test, in seven days may break at 2,970, indicating that the concrete was almost cured to the required **test strength.**

What strength concrete should you use in your house? I have only found it necessary to use 2500 psi and 3000 psi in residential work. If you want to waste your money on over kill then that is your prerogative. But after being so diligent in getting cost effectiveness into all aspects of the plan that is possible, are you going to blow the savings on something nobody can see?

Reinforcing Steel:

If concrete is so strong, why does it need reinforcing steel? Steel is used to give concrete other kinds of strength that are not inherent to its nature. If we make beams out of it, that have to span open spaces, we want it to have flexibility and tinsel strength, so it will flex without failing.

Reinforcing steel strengthens footing concrete so that the footings will be able to hold up greater weight than if there was no steel in them. The steel also transmits (spreads) these loads along the length of the footings keeping the concrete from separating, or breaking.

You may see some numbers on your foundation plan that looks like this:

4-#5 cont. This means that there will be 4 number 5 steel reinforcing bars running continuously through the footing, etc.. Number 5 steel is just like saying 5/8" diameter. If it were number 6 **bars**, they would be equal to 6 eights or ¾". The bar number is equal to eights of an inch. Example: # 7 bar = 7/8".

Footings:

As the word would suggest, footings are at the foot or bottom of the foundation. They consist of a mass of concrete and reinforcing steel in various widths and depths, depending what kind of weight (loading) will be placed on upon them.

Some other types of footings are called **piers.** They are used to support columns or concentrated loads and are sized according to how much weight they will have to support, forever.

That kind of weight, the kind that will be there as long as the building exists, is called the **dead load.** Those same structural elements that make up the **dead load** will have to support another kind of load. That is called the **live load.** This means the *movable* things that are placed in the building, something that can be taken out of the building as well. Furniture, appliances, clothing and personal possessions, etc.

PART 6
Concrete Block Construction

Concrete Block Walls:

Masonry Units:

This is the traditional concrete block, very common in many types of construction. Your basement walls may be concrete block. Many houses have concrete block exterior walls. You may see the abbreviation M.U. on your foundation plan or floor plan. It means masonry unit, which is concrete block.

The most common size M.U. is referred to as 8"x8"x16". This is a **nominal size**. The actual size would be 7-5/8"x7-5/8"x15-5/8".

Why those dirty.......! Nobody has ever called my office about the actual size of concrete blocks yet. I wonder why?

Isn't this fun? You have the inside scoop on a lot of stuff now.

Pre-cast Concrete Lintels:

Lintels are concrete beams. Some are made in a factory (pre-fabricated) and are used to span openings in concrete block (masonry) walls such as widow and door openings. The pre-fabs also serve as a concrete form. The pre-cast lintel is partially hollow and fills up with concrete when the **tie beams** are poured.

Tie Beams:

This is a concrete structure that is formed and poured as part of a concrete block wall (in residential work) to strengthen the walls and tie them together. Sometimes it is formed as the final two courses (rows) of block at the top of the wall (poured in place). Another device similar to lintels is often used for the tie beam. It is called lintel block or 'U' block because it resembles that letter when the solid ends and middle web of the blocks are knocked out so that it will form a continuous beam when filled with concrete.

Fill Cells:

The hollow openings in concrete blocks are referred to as cells or cavities. Some of them are filled with concrete and reinforced with steel to strengthen the concrete block walls.

Parge Coat:

Concrete block walls built below grade usually have a thin coat of mortar cement applied to their exterior. After it becomes hardened, a waterproofing of some variety is sprayed or rolled over it, to help prevent leakage through the walls.

Stucco Over Block:

Houses built with concrete block exterior walls frequently have stucco applied over the block to give the walls a smooth or textured finish. The stucco can then be painted with a good masonry paint to add style and color. Note: If you **are not** applying stucco to block walls and intend to paint them 'as is', I recommended you use a good block filler/primer before applying any finish paint. Consult your paint dealers for information as to the most effective products to use.

Basement Walls of Concrete Block:

One of the most common types of basement wall construction. Since basements are substantially below grade, and have the weight of the earth pressing against them, they should consist of something heavy and strong enough to withstand the pressure exerted on them from the surrounding earth.

I would suggest using a 12" concrete block in below grade applications since the added 4" of width will add to the strength of the walls. 12" block are a ***nominal*** 12" wide, 8" high and 16" long. The cells are larger and can accommodate more concrete in each **fill cell**. Your architect or designer will specify the locations and numbers of filled cells and the size of the steel reinforcing to be used.

Crawl Space Walls of Concrete:

In many areas of the country, poured concrete walls are the more traditional method of creating basements and crawl space walls. I do not advance any argument in favor of one over the other. It is a matter of cost and personal preference that determine what you use block or poured walls for your project.

Stem Walls on Footings:

These walls are concrete block built on top of a footing, but they do not extend to the vertical heights as do basement walls. They occur below grade, in the finished construction. They can be from one to several courses (rows) high, but unlike a basement these walls will have earth in between them and then concrete (floating slab) will be poured on top of the earth and between and even with the top course (row) of blocks.

Now that is a mouth full. The next paragraph will enlighten.

Stem Walls for Crawl Space:

This is like a low headroom space under the house. It is called a crawl space because you usually have to crawl to get around in it. There is no dirt fill in between the block walls, and the floor of the crawl space may be crushed stone or roughly finished concrete. Then the floor built on top of the walls will most likely be wood frame construction.

Monolithic Slab:

As the word implies, something large and powerful that acts as a single unified force. The footing and the slab, together with any other related concrete structures required within the foundation are poured all at the same time, *in one piece.* This is not only one of the most **cost effective** foundations, but one of the most expedient methods of building a foundation as well.

This slab is designed to take the loading of whatever type walls you have specified. You can use concrete block, wood frame, steel or a combination of all three.

Structural Integrity:

Another major advantage of the **monolithic slab** is **structural integrity**. *SOUNDNESS.* Just as simple as that! One piece. The fewer joints, connections, splices, etc. the greater the **structural integrity.**

Structural integrity is the name of the game. When all parts of a structure are adequately tied together in the most effective manner, you have accomplished this most important aspect of **soundness**.

I have described what I consider to be the most common and practiced methods of building foundations in the preceding paragraphs. There are other more sophisticated foundations/slabs that are rarely used in residential work, and while they are interesting, you are not likely to venture the extra money just to be different. You may even find a primitive method of providing footings if you looked closely at some old log cabin in a remote part of the woods and found the walls resting on wood timbers.

Bald Cypress, Black Locust and Eastern Cedar timbers were commonly used as foundations for houses in the southern U. S. before concrete was readily available.

PART 7
Wood Frame Construction

Wood frame has been a popular format for residential construction since the days of the colonial settlers. Back then is was a plentiful resource and one of the easiest building materials to acquire. Over the centuries, wood has maintained its popularity in home construction for a variety of reasons.

Let's take a look at some of those reasons and examine them more closely.

Wood is flexible. It can bend more easily than concrete or steel and then regain its original form. In other words it gives. You will notice this difference if you have occasion to walk on a wood floor as opposed to concrete for a prolonged period of time. The resilience of the wood will be most appreciated by your feet.

Wood is strong and lightweight. It is relatively easy to lift and handle.

Wood is easily fastened to other wood and wood structures can be assembled during most weather conditions without adverse effects.

Wood is durable, and can be made even more so by chemical treatment.

Wood is readily available, and can be transported easily.

Wood is warm. It is a natural insulator.

Wood is beautiful and practical at the same time.

Wood is competitively priced as a building material.

Wood structures go together faster.

There is another angle to the flexibility of wood that I personally like very much. It is simple to change or alter something made from wood by comparison to many other building materials.

The Floor Wafer (Deck):

The first piece of wood that goes on top of the foundation wall is called a **sill plate**. It is bolted down to the block/concrete by means of steel bolts that have been embedded into the concrete on the top of the wall. The **floor joists** are then placed on top of the **sill plate** at the designated spacing, to span the open area below.

45

Note: I frequently use the term 'member' or 'framing member' to describe any piece of lumber used in the framing process.

Floor Joists:

Usually the largest of the framing members because they do a very important job. That job is to carry all the dead and live loads placed upon them, for as long as the building lasts. There is another member placed at the ends of the joists that forms the rim of the **floor wafer.** It is called the **rim beam** or sometimes referred to as a **sill.**

Floor Trusses:

An engineered **factory fabricated structural component** designed to span long distances. They are also capable of accommodating heavy loading and resemble the superstructure of a bridge. There are many other types of components that do the same work as floor trusses and are much lighter in weight for ease of handling.

Blocking:

Blocking members are used to help hold the floor joists in vertical position so that they do not have a tendency to curl or cup (warp). They will consist of pieces of wood the same depth as the floor joists and are cut to fit tightly between the joists in a continuous row at or near the middle of the span. They also help to transmit loads placed upon them, distributing some of the weight to adjacent members.

Bridging or X-Bridging:

These member also occur in the middle of the span. They serve a similar function as blocking but are two pieces of wood or metal that hold the joists in a vertical position. They form the letter X between the joists because of the pattern in which they are nailed.

Sub Floor:

The next application is the material that covers the floor joists. This is often called decking, and can consist of laminated products like plywood or solid wood boards. The edges of either of these products may be tongue and groove (T&G). This means they will interlock so that each component will lend support to the adjacent piece, resulting is a very sturdy sub floor.

Bearing Partitions:

Partitions are an assembly of 2x4's or larger members that enclose spaces at the perimeter and within the house. **Bearing partitions** mean that these walls will be built to support some type of loads from above. They have to hold up other **dead loads**. The exterior walls of a house are most often **bearing partitions** (walls).

Non-Bearing Partitions:

You guessed it. These walls just separate the spaces you call a floor plan. They support no loads from above.

Plates:

There are plates on the bottom and top of partitions. The bottom plate is often referred to as the **sole** plate or the **shoe**. Both are different names for the same thing. I have not heard of top plates being call anything but top plates. There are two top plates on **bearing partitions**, and only one is required for **non-bearing** walls.

Studs:

The vertical members in a partition are called studs. (Not to be confused with any 'macho' carpenters on the job.) They, together with plates, form the walls, which divide the spaces into exterior walls and a floor plan.

Headers:

This device is really a wood beam and functions much like the pre-fabricated lintels we talked about in concrete block walls. When a space is required in a load-bearing wall, for doors or windows, then something is needed to span the opening and hold up the load from above.

Headers are made from wood members. They can be made up on the job site, which is often the case. Two pieces of 2x8 or larger dimension lumber, are fastened together for this purpose. However there are pre-fabricated products of great strength ready to use. They only need to be cut to the required length for the opening to be spanned.

Headers are also used in other locations. You will become aware that they are very important when an opening is necessary in a floor or roof. Examples of this application are openings for stairwells and sky-lites.

Point Loads:

This means a concentrated load being placed onto a very small area. If a **point load** is required to land on a surface that is suspended over a span, then another type of header device may be required to carry the **point load.**

This may consist two or more floor joists to be grouped together into a header or beam, to carry the **point load** across the span. You may use a manufactured component to accomplish this task. As mentioned earlier, Parallam™ is a product that is ideal for this type of application.

Ceiling Joists:

Similar to floor joists these members are used when a flat ceiling is desired. They are placed on top of the top plates of the partitions, much like the floor joists of a second story. In one story construction, ceiling joists are not required if vaulted (slopping) or cathedral ceilings are desired.

Rafters:

These are the members that makeup your roof structure. They are most frequently placed on an angle, giving the roof of the building slope, for rainwater runoff.

Roof Trusses:

An engineered **factory fabricated component** used to build roof structures. These lightweight structures are capable of spanning long distances and have been commonly in use since the 50's.

The truss technology enables roof structures to be assembled very rapidly, with little or no field cutting required as in conventional roof framing. They can be designed to accommodate a wide range of architectural styling and configurations.

Ridge:

There is a framing member at the very top of the roof, where the rafters meet that is called the **ridge**. It is sometimes referred to as the ridge board or the ridgepole.

Roof Sheathing:

This is the layer of material that is applied to the top of the rafters to complete the roof structure. It can be of plywood, or other laminated products, as well as solid wood. This process of sheathing is very similar to the sidewall sheathing that is applied to the exterior of the exterior walls.

Dry In:

You probably know what tarpaper is. The dry in is exactly that. But the construction industry likes to call it 'felt paper' or 'felts'. It is a vapor barrier to help prevent moisture penetration through the roof sheathing or sidewall sheathing. (Skin)

Flashing:

No! This is not someone giving a peek show. **Flashing** in this instance is metal, although I have used some metallic coated fabric in the past. These metals are used in places on the roof that require a very durable, long lasting material to keep water from leaking through your roof, walls, chimneys, plumbing vents, etc.

There is a type of flashing used at the eave of your roof called **edge metal** or **drip edge**. It is there to prevent leakage through the outside edge of your roof. **Flashing** is installed before the finished roof is applied over the **dry-in.** These metal protectors are also used over doors and windows, and at other potential problem areas in exterior walls to prevent leakage.

If you have ever noticed plumbing pipes coming up through a roof and seen something metallic around them, that's a type of flashing. And I'm sure you have noticed flashing where chimneys project through roofs.

Roof & Attic Ventilation:

This is a very important aspect of keeping your home cooler especially in the warmer climates. Let me explain.

Roofs and attic spaces need to be ventilated. Heat can be trapped in these spaces. If it has no way of escaping, it will expand and force its way down through the ceilings of the house. You come home from work and the house is hot. You open all the windows but the house is still uncomfortable.

The ventilation I am referring to here is not the fans you have inside your home. The problems arise from enclosed spaces over living areas that absorb heat and have no way of expelling it. If not properly ventilated these spaces will pass the heat into your living areas even if you have insulation.

We let the hot air escape through ventilating devices the are not fans. Many homes have ventilated **soffits**. This is the underside of the roof structure (rafters) that overhangs the outside walls of a house (**eaves**). Little holes or screens in the **soffits** let air in. Now let's take a look at the higher parts of the house and roof. If we can create some openings up there to let the hot air out, then we have something good going for ourselves.

Hot air rises. As it travels upward it draws cooler air with it from below. Now if that hot air has someplace to escape, we have circulation. Once we have circulation we have it made.

The roof of your house, on a warm summer day can absorb and hold tremendous heat. Dark color roofing materials get hotter than light colors. Roof wafer temperatures can reach 140 degrees or more! You certainly do not want anything like those temperatures in your house.

The solution begins at the lowest part of your roof, the **eaves**. Ventilation in the form of screen vents or perforated **soffits** are installed to allow air to enter the spaces over the insulation and between your rafters. The high part of the building is then ventilated with **ridge vents, roof vents,** and/or **gable vents**.

They all do the same job, but look different and are located differently on the roof or gable wall. **Ridge vents** are placed directly over the ridge of the roof (highest point). These are the most effective. They consist of a sheet metal fabrication, low in profile that can be connected together into a continuous ventilator along the entire length of your roof.

The **roof vent** is another sheet metal fabrication that is placed over a hole cut into the highest part of the roof. It functions much the same way as the **ridge vent** but several are needed to allow good air flow. They are much more evident and less attractive than **ridge vents.**

Gable vents are devices placed in the gable walls of your home to allow the hot air to escape from the roof wafer/attic space.

Turbine ventilators are little mechanical devices placed on roofs to extract hot air by creating a suction. When there is little or no wind, these seemingly adequate ventilators are not effective because they must rely on wind force to operate and expel hot air.

Roof exhaust fans are far and away the most effective of roof/attic ventilation. There are many very good types on the market that are energy efficient and are controlled by thermostats that turn them on and off automatically as needed.

Siding and Exterior Trim:

The cosmetics of your home. The face you will look at for many years. They are extremely important because they are the character of your home. They make others see the style and design features your architect/designer has worked to create.

There are many excellent kinds of siding on the market today. Wood, laminates, plastics, authentic colonial and Victorian products, metals and vinyl. The choices are a wonderful opportunity for you to expound on your home styling theme.

Exterior trim and bric-a-brac are another way for you to enhance the architectural style of your home. Again, the choices are now greater than ever.

Brick/stone veneer is another way of adorning the exterior of your home with color and texture. The varieties are almost endless. Whether you will have all brick, or stone, on all or part of the exterior, these products can create great impact. I like both to emphasize style on the interior by using brick or stone other than on fireplaces. I will explain a little later.

Stairs and Staircases:

Here comes another biggie. This is one of the most important singular parts of a house. It is mandatory to make it safe, for the wellbeing of yourself, your family and anyone who may ever visit your home. The building codes everywhere dictate very explicit standards for stairs.

The most often missed opportunity for giving a home that extra clincher of styling, is the staircase. The one potential feature that can be as memorable as a priceless antique, or as sensational as an original painting. It is not only functional but can be the most exciting and beautiful focal point of an otherwise ho hum house. It is the most important piece of *furniture* in your home!

If you are knowledgeable about stairs, please bear with me while I explain the nomenclature of a simple straight run staircase. There are many spectacular types of stairs that have many more parts, and many more names of parts. But let's just take the easy path, and if any of you want to get into the subject more technically then you can contact several of the companies that specialize in building staircases. I'm sure your local library can supply you with a great deal of information too.

I will name the basic parts and explain them to the best of my ability.

Stringer:

These are the side rails of the stairs. They will hold up the entire system, of all the other parts. Wide stairs often have a stringer under the middle of the staircase to give extra support. This middle member is called a **stair carriage.**

Treads:

This is what most people call the step, the part you step on to climb the stairs. On a straight **run** stairs, all treads should be the same width. The horizontal distance that the staircase occupies is called the **run**.

Riser:

This is the vertical piece of wood that you can see holding up the treads as you climb the stairs. It keeps your foot from going under the treads. There are some types of stairs that do not have risers, but the height between the top of one tread and the top of another is called the **rise or riser** even when there is no vertical piece of wood there.

The vertical distance occupied by the staircase from one floor to the next is also called the **rise**. This may sound confusing when the same word is used to describe two different situations. Just think of up. Whether it is up one step or fifteen, it is still up. Likewise with treads. They each project a certain horizontal distance, and all combined account for the stair **run**.

Building codes require uniform height for **risers** and uniform widths for **treads**. When you climb or descend a stairs you establish a rhythm. Any deviation in the rhythm caused by irregular **rise** or **run** could cause you to stumble or loose your balance. Improperly built stairs are hazardous. Many household accidents occur on stairs.

Railings:

This is where you can get artistic. Railings are fence-like devices that keep people from falling off an open sided staircase. Sometimes these railings are referred to as guardrails. They protect the open side(s) of stairs.

Railings consist of two main elements. The vertical pieces are called by different names meaning the same parts. Pickets or **balusters**, are the parts that extend from the tread up to the **handrail.** There are many unique styles of **baluster.**

Balustrade:

This is the plural for baluster. The total number of all the balusters collectively is called the **balustrade.**

Handrail:

As the word infers, this is the part of the railing that you grasp with your hand. There are many unique styles of **handrails.** Some **handrails** are installed on walls enclosing all or part of a staircase. They are mounted to the wall(s) with brackets. There are a variety of moldings used to finish stairs. You may hear such words as cove mold, and stringer mold. Just things that cover the cracks.

PART 8
Imagination is Free

Imaginative Ideas and Creativity:

The Formula for Good Style at a Good Price

I'm going to tell you a story about a model home I built early in my construction career. This was in a subdivision where sales had been very sluggish, and only three houses had been built there in the first sixteen months since the subdivision had been opened. Other custom home developments in the high price ranges abounded in this area, and most were enjoying steady business.

I selected a split site lot, one that was a fairly level half way to the rear lot line, and then a fairly steep incline to another gentle slope that ended at the rear of the lot. It was perfect for a walkout basement! And there were several more lots just like it so I could duplicate this walkout basement idea in a variety of other locations.

The new model would be a two story house, built over a daylight basement. I got together with the architect and formulated a plan. I wanted to make this house really different but I had to stay within the budget. What could be done to make this model unlike all the others being built in the area. How could I make it stand out above other two story houses?

The architect suggested a curved staircase, but that was a budget buster. Curves are costly. But what if I made two straight stair sections look like a curve. I could make the shape of the entrance foyer a blunted diamond instead of an oval. Then by placing two winder treads (wedge shaped) between the straight sections I could create the illusion of a curve without having to pay big bucks for the real thing. I talked to my stair builder and he made another suggestion that carried the illusion of a curved staircase a bold step farther.

We would rack the two straight sections. Let me explain in simple terms. A straight section staircase forms a rectangle. You can change that shape to a parallelogram by moving the stringers. Then all the treads would become parallelograms too. This would take very little more materials to create the winder treads, otherwise the budget would not change.

Another idea was foremost in my mind. I wanted to do something really different with a kitchen. A departure from the traditional. I had seen a photo of a fireplace built from old stone pavers that had been removed from the bed of a trolley car track. But where would I ever find anything like that? And at what cost?

I arranged to meet my fireplace mason, Jack, at the biggest brickyard in town. We were discouraged to discover nothing in the way of reclaimed pavers. The owner of the company had not seen anything like that around for years.

We pacified ourselves by walking around the brickyard looking at everything they had. Nothing appealed, nothing excited. Just lots of different colored bricks!

Well, on to another place. But just as we were about to depart, I noticed a large silhouette near the railroad siding. "What's under that tarp?" I asked.

"Oh, that's a pile of leftover brick from the community college job we supplied. I have to keep them covered because they are a very porous pressed brick, not fired like other brick. They are a big pain to work with too. Nobody wants them."

I decided to take a look. There it was. Better than I could have imagined. A soft red color range, larger than regular brick. It was called a Norman brick. 2-1/2" thick, five inches wide, and 14" long. Jack got the drift of my thinking and began stacking a mock up wall, just to see how they looked.

I did the same, but instead of piling the brick in the usual fashion, I stood my pile up on edge, so that you saw the face that was usually covered. Just what I wanted. I would have something that looked like the old pavers. 5"x14" and they were intentionally made to look rustic and irregular. I was elated! Little did I realize what a trend I was starting in fireplace face brick.

Jack was jubilant. He was a master fireplace builder, always wanting to do something new and exciting. He was anxious to get started. I knew we had a winner in the starting gate.

I had my different kitchen. With a big fireplace, and a brick walled cooking alcove next to it, my country kitchen was the talk of the town.

People were asking what this new product was. They had never seen anything like it. And all we did was stand brick up on edge.

The staircase was awesome. People saw it as a curve. The balusters were very different too. We cut a simple pattern out of the middle of 10" wide cedar boards like those used in Swiss Chalets. And we cut decals out of 1/8" laminate and planted one on the face of every riser on the staircase. The effect was most dramatic.

The first thirty days after the opening of the model home I had taken reservations on ten of the remaining 22 lots.

I had taken something no one wanted, used it differently than people were used to seeing it, and created something 'NEW'! **Imagination!**

The owner of the brick company called me one day soon after the beginning of this promotion. He said several people wanted to buy the remaining inventory of Norman brick I had purchased from him for use in my model home. He offered to reserve the entire supply of my 'discovery' exclusively for my use. All I had to do was say yes.

YES!

We all have creativity in us. It just takes some stimulus to get us thinking, some reasons to use our talents. You can acquire this kind of sense once you begin looking at things. It's really quite easy.

Interior Finishing:

Electrical, Plumbing, Heating/Air Conditioning:

Who Gets Priority?
Once the roofing is completed and the building is weather tight you are ready for the trades. I make it a practice to get the ductwork necessary for heating and air conditioning installed first.

Ductwork takes a good deal more space than plumbing and wiring, so I give this trade first shot. Why? If the rough plumbing and wiring are in place first, they could easily block the areas best suited for ductwork. Airflow is critical if your system is going to give you satisfactory service. It can have the first priority because wiring and plumbing installations are more flexible.

I will not elaborate on the trades any more than to say they are each worthy of a separate book. These installations each require their own codes, and are closely regulated. They are also subject to very rigid inspections by people proficient in those trades, and who are very knowledgeable in their requirements.

Insulation:

Once the trades have all passed inspection, then you may insulate and close in the walls. Many building departments require insulation inspection before the drywall process begins.

Insulation is one of the few products I can think of that will eventually pay for itself. Of course like with anything else you can over do it. Some people use 2x6 studs in the exterior walls just to accommodate more insulation. I do not discourage this idea, however if you are anxious about energy costs, and freezing conditions or extreme heat because of where you are going to be living, then I find nothing wrong with playing it safe.

There are many types of insulation on the market. They all function about the same except some are more efficient, easier to handle and install. The foam insulators are being recognized as the most efficient of products available for residential use. They are more cumbersome to handle because they are rigid and cannot be compressed for shipping like fiberglass and mineral wool that are packages in rolls.

I have not seen foam insulation in wide use as yet in housing, except for companies that make wall panels which integrate the foam insulators as part of the manufacturing process. These companies are basically house prefabricators. I am not referring to anything like mobile home manufacturers. That is a completely different type of product that is not part of the discussions in this book.

You will need to explore the system which fits your needs and budget, and hopefully you will make a wise decision. I would encourage you to investigate the possibilities of Styrofoam, polystyrene foam or other insulators of this nature. If there is an insulation contractor in your community who is familiar with this type installation you may be in luck.

R-Factor:

What is an R factor? The term means **thermal resistance factor**. In simple definition, how much heat/cold it will keep from penetrating. You will see numbers like R-11, R-19, R-40. They are related to a theoretical comparison of how many feet of earth it would take to develop a particular

thermal resistance. In theory, if you piled six feet of earth on top of your house, your roof would have a thermal resistance value of R-40.

Drywall:

When I first entered the construction industry this was a dirty word. Drywall technology was not very advanced, and was not well known to do-it-yourselfers. Because it was much less expensive many hearty souls attempted to install their own, and many botched jobs gave this excellent and practical product a bad rap. True, there were technical problems, especially in the fastening systems and joint treatment used then.

The public resisted this product for many years. Selling drywall in new homes was a tough nut. But just imagine the alternative. Plaster, which while being the tradition took many weeks to accomplish, was much more labor intensive, and did some nasty things to the house in which it was being installed.

Drywall is sheets of plaster made in a factory. It has a skin (paper) to keep it from coming apart while being handled. It has become the most common interior wall and ceiling material used in construction. It is relatively inexpensive, installs quickly, and reduces the construction schedule by many days, even weeks.

Plaster:

Picture yourself going out to find and purchase good lumber for your new home. You wanted to be certain that is was kiln dried and well cured, because there was a great deal of green lumber on the market in those days, and green lumber was responsible for numerous problems in new homes.

You found the quality you wanted and proceeded with the framing process then had all the trades completed, and next was the plasterer. (Insulation was not even required in the old days.) First came the lathers. These workers had the job of installing the material onto which the plaster was applied. Lath was no longer made from wood and wire, but a new product called rock-lath was going to be used on your house. It was very similar to drywall but was installed in pieces that were 16" wide and 4 feet long.

These guys tied up your job for the best part of a week. They left it looking like white chalk was crumbled on the floors, and all your beautiful lumber was covered with a hodge-podge of random pieces of something unsightly.

A few days later, the plastering crew showed up with a truckload of planks and scaffolding, barrels, hoses, mixing tubs, and all kinds of funny looking tools. Then another truck pulls up and unloads a zillion bags of plaster coat, and lots of sand, and lots of other funny looking tools. They even brought a couple of wheelbarrows.

The next day you can't even walk through your own house because there is so much stuff in the way and a lot of very rough looking guys. 'Geez', you say to yourself, 'I don't think I wanna go in there with that bunch around!'

You go back a few days later and see a dark brown mess on the walls and wonder what's going on. Isn't plaster supposed to be white?

'It's the scratch coat', the foreman tells you. 'We call it the brown coat too, because of the color. Some people call it the ground coat, but it's just the first layer to go on.'

It takes another week before you see real white plaster going onto the walls. But the place is a wreck. There is dirt, and sand and plaster dust (white) all over everything. And the water! All the beautiful dry lumber is getting soaked! Water is being spilled everywhere.

Another week goes by and you go back to find the foreman working in the same spot he was in the last time you were there. When are these guys ever going to be finished, you wonder. It seems like they have been here forever.

The foreman is rubbing some little wooden tool over and over on the same spot, and then throwing water on it and doing the whole process over again.

I actually recollect scenes like this in my early years, and I don't think I could tolerate the extra labor and time added to a construction schedule anymore.

Things always go much slower that I would like and I would probably have a nervous breakdown if I saw some laborer forget that the hose in the full barrel of water was still turned on and the barrel was overflowing onto my nice dry plywood sub-floor. One's constitution does weaken with age.

Stucco:

Although this is basically a plastering process, it is most likely to take place on the outside of a building. The mess doesn't seem so bad out of doors. I like stucco and have used this product to cover the exterior of concrete block houses by the zillions.

Interior Finishing:

Doors and Millwork:

This subject is vast, and I think most people know what a door is. So let's just tiptoe through it and touch on a few things that might keep you out of the pit.

Pre-hung doors are very popular. They have already been attached to the hinges and jambs (frames) in a factory and are very easy and quick to install. They are made from wood or composition material such as masonite. There is a great variety of styles available making it easy to establish a theme in your home.

Exterior doors are also pre-hung. Many are made from metal and have special qualities because they are insulated and do not warp or rot like wood. They are called thermal doors because they are insulated and protect the entrances of your house from heat and cold. Many are equipped with special adjustable thresholds to seal the bottom of the door when it is closed. This insures a weather tight seal from the elements. The styles available are dazzling.

Casings, Moldings and Baseboard:

These molding come in many styles to help you continue your theme ideas to the last detail. The casings are used to trim around doors and windows. The baseboard is used to finish the walls at the floor line. Baseboard and casings are made in two formats. Finger-jointed and solid wood. Finger jointed means a long length of wood molding may consist of a series of small pieces joined together. It is the more economical of the two and is generally used if painted woodwork is specified. If you intend to stain your woodwork you will prefer solid wood trim.

Cabinetry:

Your choices will be vast. Cabinetry is an industry in itself. Cabinets are like furniture, as well as being functional. Together with the counter tops they add style and color to a home.

Floor Coverings:

Many homeowners like more than one kind of floor covering in their home. Because some parts of a home are used for different functions, many of those rooms may need something special. Bathrooms frequently have ceramic tile floors to cope with moisture situations inherent in bathrooms. Kitchens likewise are special use areas. You may desire vinyl, ceramic tile, carpet or wood. There are beauty and durability aspects to consider.

Pit:

I have had people insist on hardwood flooring in kitchens. It looks very charming but there is undue risk involved. One such client insisted, so I made him sign a release that held me harmless forever should the floor buckle. On the fifth day after they moved in, his daughter spilled a whole pitcher of lemonade on the kitchen floor. It was a disaster!

Pit:

One other floor covering presents problems to some homeowners. That is vinyl. Especially the very high gloss (wet look) styles. They are beautiful, but two problems plague many people who select this usually expensive product. Vinyl flooring cuts and is ripped very easily. It also shows the slightest imperfections of the surfaces on top of which it is installed, due to its great resilience.

Painting and Wall Coverings:

Color, color, color. Important, important, important! Color can make things look bigger or smaller. Bright or gloomy. Warm, cold, cheerful, sterile, dirty, serene, brilliant, *even sexy.* We could go on with many more adjectives, because color can be likened to so many different moods.

Using color wisely can work wonders. It can be used to emphasize important statements you make throughout your home. It can bring charm into otherwise dull places. Color brings materials to life. It brings comfort into narrow places. It can be exciting. It can be artful.

I do not mean to imply that your house should be a rainbow, but don't be afraid to use color. You are going to have to pay for paint, so why not make the most of it.

Wallpaper can add color and design. Fabrics can add color and texture.

Many of these elements can be used in creative combinations. You are setting the stage for your home to come alive. It will be YOU!

Pierre Renaldo

PART 9
Federal Flood Zones

Velocity Zones:

Man has always lived near water. Man has actually spent eons in search of water, and in search of what lay beyond the water. Man wanted to be close to water. The seas, the lakes, rivers and ponds. Living beside all of these bodies of water has been a favored habitat of mankind since the beginning of time.

And then there was light, and the light shined on the water, and man liked what he saw. "I will live here forever", he said. "Water is good."

And then there was FEMA and FEMA said, "Hey man, we ain't gonna let you live *that* close to the water!"

F.E.M.A. = Federal Emergency Management Agency

A **velocity zone** is classified as a very high risk coastal area, prone to high winds with tidal surges and flooding. There are two major categories in these zones, each imposing regulations on how you can build a home therein. Each is intended to 'guide' those persons who choose to build their homes in such risky places.

These regulations restrict living conditions inside any structure below a designated height above **Mean Sea Level, (MSL).** You will see this designation on your survey if your land is in a **flood zone**. It means, the average high tide waterline over an annual time period.

Now that was a mouthful, so let me get a little detailed here. I promise not to get any more technical than it takes to explain a critically important requirement. It is mandatory, so it must be done or you will have spent a lot of money for nothing.

If you build in a **flood zone**, the U.S. Government will sell you a policy for National Flood Insurance. But the building, not yourself must qualify for this policy by conforming to the regulations set forth by FEMA. There is no way around it.

National Flood Insurance is required by any bank who may finance your construction project. It is required by the building department of jurisdiction wherein your home will be located.

Example:
Ken and Margaret bought a beautiful lot on an island off the West Coast of Florida. It was not directly on the water but was only a short distance from the beach and the Inter-Coastal Waterway and Sarasota Bay. The **flood zone** was verified to be an **A-15 Zone.** This meant that the lowest elevation of any *finished floor* in the living area of their house would have to be at least 15 feet above **Mean Sea Level (MSL).**

The survey for their lot showed the existing land to be 4.65 feet MSL. With a 15-foot elevation requirement, this meant the lowest floor in the living space of the home to be built had to be at least 10.35 feet higher than the existing grade on their lot.

The city had zoning restrictions against filling more than one foot above the crown of the road. The obvious solution was an elevated house. We would build so that the first floor living level was 15.5 MSL. Just a little extra height for good measure.

V-Zone:

This category requires the most stringent implementations. Foundations must be *driven pilings* exclusively! The elevation requirement in **V-Zones** is not to the finished floor level of the lowest habitable space, but to the height of the *lowest point of horizontal structure.* Wow! That's a big difference from an **A-Zone!**

Driven Pilings:

This is an operation requiring a pile driving crane which can virtually hammer a large wooden or concrete pole or steel beam to great depths into the earth. The depth required will depend on how soft the ground is and how much weight the pilings are going to hold. With this system the entire weight of the building will rest on the pilings once they are driven to the required depth and resistance.

There are formulas for determining how much weight the pilings will sustain once they are in place. These formulas are based the amount of friction and resistance the piling encounters during the driving process, until these desired factors are achieved. Test borings before the work is started, reveal information that the structural engineers use to make structural design determinations about the depth and size of pilings.

Note: If you intend to use the driven pilings as your finished (above grade) columns, I recommend you use the pre-stressed concrete pilings.
Wood columns tend to allow more movement (sway) during periods of brisk winds. Many people become very uncomfortable when this occurs.

Example:
Joe and Shirley bought a lot on the beach. It was located in a V-16 Zone. Their house would have to be on top of several driven pilings. As a cost saving device, the pilings used would be ordered extra length and then utilized as the finished column supports (above grade) for the elevated beams we would cast on top of them. Next we would build the floor wafer on top of those concrete beams.

A-Zone

Now here is where the big difference comes in between **V-Zone** and **A-Zone**. The bottom of the beams we would cast on top of the driven pilings, were the height required to comply with FEMA in a **V-Zone**. From the existing grade at the building site to the bottom of the lowest point of horizontal structure, not to the finished floor of the lowest habitable area! That is a difference of two feet!

Note: The federal government prohibits the use of any area of a residence, below a designated Federal Flood Zone Elevation, to be used as habitable living space. You cannot have a bedroom, or a bathroom, or any other type living condition below designated Flood Zone Elevation!

I just wanted you to realize it is serious business building in a **Flood Zone.** Many more restrictions that I will not outline here, are available from your building department. I think it is good practice to get the particulars affecting your project from the people who will be visiting your site to make sure you are in compliance with codes as well as FEMA regulations.

If all the foregoing wasn't enough, the building codes for the **Flood Zones** are more stringent too. Again be sure you have updated information affecting the design of your home. Regulations are changed constantly, so don't rely on outdated information. That can be a pit. A few months after Hurricane Andrew devastated Florida there was a whole new building code in effect.

How can anybody tell how high my house is above sea level, you may ask yourself. You must verify this information, by hiring a surveyor to establish these heights as soon as your first floor wafer is completed.

He will measure everything by instrument and then issue to you an **elevation certificate**(s), which you must present to your building department. If you are financing the project you will also be required to present your lending institution with a copy, signed and sealed by your surveyor.

Deep Pit:
Zoning restrictions vary from one community to another. Make absolutely certain you know what they are for your project. You have chosen to live there, so it is your responsibility to be familiar with how the ordinances (laws) in the place of your own choosing will affect you, your project and your lifestyle.

Case in Point:
On occasion I have built in seaside resorts that have had some unusual zoning restrictions and ordinances. Some of them have building height restrictions that at first glance seem like all the others. But when you read through them the second time you find that this particular place considers a building's height from *sea level* rather than the existing grade at the building site.

Nothing wrong with that you say to yourself. But then you look at your survey and see that little surveyor's symbol indicating that your property is Elev.7.25 MSL. The height restriction limits single family dwellings to 38 feet above MSL. And you had just decided to go ahead with the widow's watch option, that would require another 12 feet of height on your house.

Let's take a look at the height requirements for what you want to build.

You decided to build up your parking slab under the house so that it will be 2 feet higher than the crown of the road. Then you have a foundation that is 8 feet high and a floor wafer that is 12" thick. The exterior wall height of the first floor is 8 feet. The roof slope accounts for another 4 feet. Look what would happen if you added the widow's watch.

All the numbers add up to 38 feet 3 inches. No can do! But you had the foresight to check this out thoroughly before you started your project. Simply lower the roof of the widows watch by 3". And you could shave the parking slab pad by a couple more inches to be on the safe side.

There have been true-life situations, when people have discovered this horrible kind of mistake after all these heights were already in the form of a completed structure. Many dollars wasted on a not so simple oversight. If this situation occurred in a **V-Zone**, the elevation requirement would make for a very illegal tall building in a very restrictive zoning environment.

Many old beach communities wrote their ordinances long before they knew they were going to be in Federal Flood Zones. They never anticipated that what they thought were fair zoning restrictions would have a negative impact on new construction.

Warning: When you purchase an existing property to either demolish or renovate you are likely going to be subject to the latest codes/ordinances of the municipality and any applicable Flood Zone regulations. You will have to upgrade to current standards. Don't ever assume you can be 'grandfathered' in. Check it out with your building department. Get your information first hand, *only and always*.

Engineering and Other Special Requirements:

You will be required to have your working drawings reviewed by a professional engineer or a registered architect in order to obtain building permits in flood zones. The embossed seal and engineer's signature must appear on every drawing page germane to the **flood zone** regulations. You should anticipate additional expense for these services.

As I mentioned earlier, the building code requirements for **flood zone** construction are more complex. For example; any walls built to enclose the perimeter of the building that occurs below the required flood zone elevation in a **V-Zone** must be *collapsible.*

In the event of a tidal/storm surge of the sea reaching the foundation, the walls would have to be built so that they would fall free of the foundation upon wave impact. This would allow the sea to flow freely under the building for whatever length of time this flood condition existed!

In addition, these walls would have to be equipped with flow through devices that would allow inactive (standing) water to flow into and then out of the lower portions of any enclosed area at grade.

Hurricane Andrew (South Florida August 1992) and Mitch (Honduras and The Bay Islands of Guanaja and Roatan, October 1998) brought storm surges of fifteen feet when they made landfall. Fifteen feet higher than high tide!

None of these restrictions seemed to matter to people who want to live close to the water. I specialized in construction of elevated houses (platform structures) for many years in the coastal areas of Florida. There was never a lack of clients.

There may be other requirements imposed by the building department of jurisdiction. Be sure to check with them so that you are not in for more surprises.

Properties In Two Flood Zones:

If even a miniscule portion of your property falls within a more stringent flood zone category, then your entire project will be subject to higher classification of the two.

Super Pit:

Properties That Infringe on Coastal Setback Lines:

Coastal setback lines are imposed by state governments to protect wildlife, endangered vegetation, and to control coastal erosion. In the event any part of a property lies *seaward* of this line, then it will be subject to a very complex series of special regulations in addition to FEMA, applicable building codes, and all other ordinances and restrictions.

These may include requirements for special structures to cross sensitive areas (sand dunes, turtle crossings, stands of sea oats, etc.). Additional permits are required, and each case is reviewed individually. There are additional fees (non-refundable) you must pay, in addition to reams of paperwork. Your application may be denied, preventing you from building anything on the property.

There are also special engineering requirements for these circumstances. Structural engineering evaluations and calculations must be submitted with working drawings and special exhibits. A professional engineer will have to make periodic inspections of the work progress and he must submit a written report reiterating his inspection findings, at the end of each month. Of course this all costs much more money.

This permitting process sometimes takes several years. Unless you have infinite patience and a strong constitution, I suggest you pass up any property in this category.

Case History:

Betty and Byron purchased a property near the beach on a beautiful island off the West Coast of Florida. They did not intend to build on it for several years, until Byron was ready to retire. They would go there on weekends, park on their property and walk 200 feet to the beach. The property was in an **A-Zone** and they already knew about the special requirements imposed by this flood zone category.

A few years passed and suddenly on a day in August 1992, Hurricane Andrew destroyed a large portion of South Florida. A few months later the State of Florida moved the Coastal Setback Line inland two hundred feet. Most of the coastal areas affected by the setback line change were several hundred miles from where Andrew did all the damage. But the bureaucracy always knows best.

When Betty and Byron heard the news they went to the municipality building department. The new map of the areas affected, proved that 25 % of their lot was now seaward of the Coastal Setback Line. They would be subject to the most stringent regulations of all, even though they had purchased the property before the change.

They appealed to the zoning board, who was powerless to grant a variance to State and Federal requirements. Their plans would be altered considerably.

The story ended happily, but the final cost of the project was far more expensive due to an imaginary line being drawn across a portion of their land.

I have intentionally not covered every miniscule point on the subject of flood zones. I hope to entice you with enough information to make you want to know the whole story. That way you will surly go to your building department to get all the details. They will keep you from falling into a pit.

Elevated houses are challenging things to build. Once you decide to produce a home built up in the air, it becomes a completely different product than one built on the ground. There are great opportunities for doing something as different as building on a split site. And by the way, the elevated house is very adaptable to steep terrain.

Don't settle for plain vanilla. There is already too much of that flavor around, and it is terribly boring. When I pass houses that have absolutely no style I look at many missed opportunities. I guess some people just don't care about looks.

PART 10
Wrapping It Up

What Happens When the Work is Completed:

We have come to the end of one road and the beginning of another. Now you are really getting excited about moving into your dream. How wonderful it will be.

But there are still some little details to be resolved. And we want to make sure everything is in good working order.

Walkthrough and Punch-out:

This process is a check of all the things in your home. You schedule an appointment with your builder and proceed to review every room in the house. Notations are made about any missing bits and pieces, the appliances and equipment are checked to make sure they are operational. The punch-out is completed in a few days and then you actually move in.

It's hard to believe the whole thing is over. It has actually been fun, even exciting. The routine of visiting the construction site every day is over.

You will not have to travel to see your house daily because you will be living there.

Warranty Registration:

There will be warranties to be reviewed, registrations to fill out and send in. You should do this quickly, so you don't forget. Some of the major appliance manufacturers have automatic warranty registration, so you don't have to do anything about them except read the owner's manuals.

Make up a file for all your warranty papers. If you don't already know all the phone numbers to call in case of problems or need of information, make sure you get that list.

Warranty Services:

Keep a little poster on the inside of a kitchen cabinet door, listing all the numbers you may need, including emergency numbers. The poster should list information about you and your house. Address, phone number, builders name, name of subdivision and lot number if applicable.

Many of the people who have contributed to the completion of your home have been using the lot number as the address during the construction process, so have it handy just in case.

Report any problems quickly and accurately. When you call for any kind of service, try to give a concise explanation of the problem. This will insure the most expedient repairs, and no wasted trips. Time is money to the trades people who will be responding to your requests. The company they work for may bill you if unnecessary trips are required to fix something you reported in error.

Every home needs to go through a break-in period. After you have had enough experience with your new home, then review any minor problems with the appropriate trades people for service.

When you make appointments with service people, make sure someone is home to let them in, and to show them the problem. Likewise, get them to commit to a time frame so that you don't have to waste a whole day waiting for someone who cannot get to your house until late afternoon.

Delays are inevitable because service personnel are frequently involved with 'unanticipated complications.' Though at times it may be difficult, patience will always be a virtue. Keep your cool.

PART 11
Some Innermost Secrets

Digging Your Own Pit:

Starting off on the Wrong Foot.

A few years ago a young man named Jerry P. came to my office with a sketch of a floor plan drawn on graph paper. He and his wife Donna had conceived a great idea for the house they wanted to build on their island lot. He informed me that the plan was "in scale" and asked me to come up with a price. He also left me with a long list of 'options' to price out for their consideration.

"I'll stop in next week", he informed me. "I come over to cut the grass on the lot every week."

At a glance I could see that the stairs drawn on his floor plan would never work. The list of options was without a doubt a 'pie in the sky' dream. They were out shopping the prices with every builder in town. I was not about to go through several hours of calculations on what I already knew was going to be a big waste of time.

Two weeks later I gave him back his plan and a ballpark number for the construction costs. I told him to come back when he had his ideas finalized, and if he had working drawings I would then take another look at his dream.

Time is money:

People do not realize how much time goes into pricing plans. A long list of options is an invitation to another such list once the first one is discarded in favor of reality. You should not expect people to enjoy wasting time giving you quotes to satisfy outlandish curiosity. I could tell that these people were a long way from getting their thoughts together. They would not be serious until they exhausted the patience of all the saints.

Knowing What You Want:

One of the greatest human failings is indecision. How much patience should a businessman have, waiting for you to decide on what you really want. Do you know what you like, or only what you don't like? Building a home is not like trying on a pair of shoes. Changes can be very expensive, and if you decide you do not like something after the fact, then you are in deep do-do.

Cheapest Price:

Remember the old saying, 'you get what you pay for!' What really is the lowest price? Do you know what is included in that low price? Does it include the things you really want? Or is it a bigger compromise than you bargained for?

Cost Per Square Foot: Real or Scam?

Here is where the fun begins. You will hear all kinds of numbers being tossed around. You just won't know if they are real. When people call and ask me how much I charge per square foot, I tell them I won't know until they tell me in detail what they want in their house. I also tell them I can build a house for $15. per square foot, but they probably would not want to live in it.

I can't think of anything more likely to alienate me from a potential client quicker than getting barraged with a lot of numbers they have heard all over town. It just gets silly and I'll explain why.

Forensic Numbers:

Given a specific plan with detailed specs, any good builder can give you a firm number. This will be an estimated number unless this plan is a repetitive production house. That means it is a stock model that is built often. The costs are well known.

One of a kind homes are not repeated. It is a one time venture and may vary radically from any other house I have ever built. I will estimate the costs and though I have a good idea how much it will cost to build, I will only know the **real numbers** after the house is completed. That is the **forensic number.**

So if Mr. P. asks me how much I charge per square foot and his house is unlike anything I have done before, then I can only estimate the costs.

Square Footage Pit:

What Is The Square Footage Of a Building?

Here is how many people are fooled. But many of them dig this pit for themselves, shopping for the lowest cost per square foot number. Here is how it happens.

Does the square foot number include just living spaces? How about attached garages, porches, sun decks and concrete patios.? Do they count? Would it cost more to build a roof with three-foot overhangs than a roof with one-foot overhangs? Does a steep roof take more materials and labor than a shallow slope? You already know the answers.

Areas Under Roof:

Everything counts! All areas under the roof, or isolated structures, no matter what their function will cost money. They are all part of the total square footage of the building.

The Saga Of Donna P.

Mrs. Donna P. is determined to find the lowest price for her building plans. Her house plan consists of two stories in height, with a big verandah on the front and a screened porch off the first floor rear. There is an open sundeck above the screened porch accessible from the master bedroom on the second floor. And she would like a little gazebo and a patio in the yard off the screened porch.

Builder Z states over the phone that his houses run about $58 per square foot. Mrs. P. does a quick calculation in her head. She has found a sleeper. She tells her husband that he has been talking to all the wrong people. She has found the best deal in town. This is exciting she tells herself.

They go to builder Z's office, have a good chat and leave their plans. But when the price quote comes in it is not $58. per square foot. How come?

Mrs. P. is very unhappy. She and her husband have a conference with builder Z. He states that the type homes he builds do not have verandahs or screened porches with gazebos, patios and sun decks. So these items have to be added to the $58. price. After all they cost a lot of money. They cannot be built for free.

It wasn't long before my telephone was ringing. You guessed it. Donna P. was calling in a huff. "What do you charge per square foot for a two story house?" She thinks I'm going to be sucked in to this game she wants to play.

"I have already given your husband an estimate. You can do the arithmetic yourself. I have never seen anything but a rough sketch of your idea, and I'm not even going to venture a wild guess over the telephone. You may have added many things to the plans which I have never seen yet."

She was angry. Nobody was stupid enough to loose money to build her house. She had not yet found the dummy she was sure she would find sooner or later. Her husband brought the plans to my office that afternoon. They could come by in two days and I would have a price ready.

Upon entering my office the first thing Donna blurted out was, "We are definitely going with the person who quotes us the lowest price!" She had put me on notice that if I didn't come in with a low enough number to suite her she would go out and find some dummy who would. I rolled up the plans and handed them to her.

"Sorry, Donna, that person will not be me. Good luck."

She did eventually find somebody. Six months after she moved into her new house she put it on the market and moved back to the mainland. She hated her house! It didn't turn out anything like she had envisioned, and she hated the builder too.

Don't Play Games:

Anybody who has been in the construction business for any length of time can spot the players. I don't think any builder wants to waste time with people who think they have figured out a way to sneak one in on somebody.

And when a prospect hands me a list of twenty 'options' he wants priced, I just hand it back to him and suggest he check these things out with Home Depot.

Game players do not get the best deals on price. The builder will expect this pattern of behavior to continue throughout the project if he takes it on, and build in an extra margin against the possibility of trickery.

THE GOLDEN RULE IS ONE OF THE MOST IMPORTANT THINGS TO REMEMBER WHEN YOU ARE INVOLVED WITH BUSINESS DEALING OF ANY KIND! Personal integrity will get you much more than playing games. You will have the respect of those you deal with and gain far more than if you attempt any kind of deception.

Be A Good Business Person:

A good business association should be just that. Business! If you enter into an agreement with anyone for any kind of goods or services it should be with the understanding that the product or service is what you are purchasing. You are not buying people.

Do not do business with people whom you do not trust. You will never be happy with those individuals even if they are honest. **Mutual trust is the ingredient essential to good business relationships.**

Be Truthful And Candid:

Say what you feel, and say what you think. It is always better to get your feelings out in the open. You will only be working against yourself if you hold back or try to mask your concerns until it is too late. If you do not understand something or you think something is in error, get it resolved quickly. Be comfortable with all the facts up front.

Negotiate Honestly:

This is your best chance to get the most for the money you spend. Be realistic in your position. Don't expect someone to give away the store just to get your business. People have the perception that builders make gigantic profits on every job. That may have happened long ago, but modern day businesses survive because they give good value. Risk factors are enormous and insurance and taxes take a hefty bite out of every transaction. They cannot sell you a house at 1965 prices and survive.

Bury the Hatchet!

Many people feel put upon once they find they cannot get the price they imagined they would like to pay. They carry a grudge, often induced by what other people have told them. You can catch more bees with honey than with vinegar. Remember that this is your project, and it doesn't have to be a fiasco just because someone you know had a bad experience.

PART 12
In Retrospect

Satisfaction:

This should be the bottom line. It is a wonderful feeling to know you have caused someone to be satisfied. And whenever that happens I have that warm fuzzy feeling myself. It becomes a mutual thing.

I'm sure you have all experienced those individuals who are never satisfied with anything. I have had my share, meaning even one is enough. These people are happy only when they are causing discomfort to others. They are critical of the most perfect things. It's just their makeup, a personality quirk.

A few years ago I had one of the most satisfying experiences of my career.

I had signed a contract with a delightful couple just going into retirement.

They had a definite idea of what they wanted, and one of my catalog designs with a few modifications would be a perfect match up.

I found these people to be most pleasant to work with and they were most receptive to my suggestions. The work progressed nicely and by late summer they moved into a home that was the most functional and dramatic house they had ever owned. It was just perfect for them and they really enjoyed the building experience, even though she was sure at the outset that it would be just another unhappy adventure for her. They were elated and most complementary to my workers and me.

A short time later I was invited to a house warming at their new residence, where Mrs. L. the owner, announced publicly that after building several homes in their lifetime, this was the only time it had been a pleasant happening. All other experiences had been distressful.

Their daughter later told me that everyone who knew Mrs. L. was certain that she and I would mix like oil and water. They were making bets that this rather outspoken and oftentimes sarcastic lady would be in serious conflict with me before the job had advanced very far.

All's well that ends well. These people have since become two of my closest personal friends.

Let's All Be On The Same Team:

This is not as difficult to accomplish as you may think. What better person to have on your team than the person who is making your dream a reality. It works. You do not have to be adversaries, and you don't have to fall in love with each other.

Your builder is the person most able to guide you to a happy fulfillment of your objectives. If you are in conflict, the end product suffers. If you treat your builder like an adversary that's what he will become.

Working together as a team does not mean you give up anything. With adequate discussion and review before the work begins you can avoid the petty conflicts (they are the pits) and misunderstandings that so often occur in business transactions. That is because the team approach keeps everyone working for the same goals. All have a thorough understanding of what is to be done, up front. This will be a great benefit to you, the proud homeowner.

Stay Positive And Focused:

There are always setbacks and delays. If everything does not go just the way you think it should, it is because that is the normal order of things. Nobody is perfect. Workers won't show, deliveries are delayed, backorders hold up the work. That's just the way the construction industry is made up. Consider that a house has over thirty thousand parts! Don't be overly excited if the plumber does not show up when he said he would. It's not the end of the world.

Don't Sweat The Flyspecks:

Trivia has a major negative impact on some people. They dwell on the most miniscule things, often completely overlooking the most important. You need to be aware of <u>all</u> events happening on your project. The nitty-gritty all comes together in the end. You should not loose sleep over the one thing that is important to you and forget the excitement of all the major processes taking place.

I have seen people actually suffer from the effects of what I call monomania.

They have concentrated their entire life on a singular small point to the exclusion of everything else going on. They miss all the fun.

One couple I built an island home for several years ago wanted a fireplace with a marble hearth. This lady had her heart set on it, and the edges of the marble that were visible around the periphery of the hearth had to be polished. This was the big event for Mrs. G.

When the marble arrived on the site, she was there to open the boxes and examine every piece to make sure the edges were polished. Much to her chagrin some of the pieces did not have polished edges. Those pieces were for interior areas of the hearth that would not have exposed edges. Mrs. G. nearly had a stroke.

This one event was all she could think about while her house was being built. I think we could have left half the roof off and she would not have noticed.

Once everything was in place on the hearth, she was happy. A girlfriend had told her to make sure the edges of her marble squares were polished, or she would have a noticeable flaw on her fireplace hearth.

Some Traditions Are Obsolete:

Contracts are written to divide. The traditional contracts between builders and clients establish two distinct sides. It seems like everybody is lining up for a fight.

That's how the lawyers make their money. Creating an adversarial relationship right from the beginning. I think this is the cause of disputes, not their resolution. Friendlier language in contracts would probably circumvent many disputes. I have found that the more simple the contract, the less problems I encounter.

The detail belongs on the plans and specifications. We should spend less time writing tricky language into the legal documents and concentrate on getting a total understanding into all the minds involved. Then building would be something enjoyable. The horror stories would end. Why make client and builder enemies on paper before the construction begins?

Truly a wacky tradition.

Good Ideas, Bad Laws:

The Florida Lien Law makes contractors in that state appears to be known criminals. Something that is supposed to protect the working man in the construction industry makes honest contractors suspect.

An owner receives a notice by Certified Mail that warns of *possible* non-payments to sub-contractors and suppliers by their builder. The way it is written makes him look like a crook. Then if you can understand the small print you find a disclaimer that states this may not necessarily apply to this particular builder. But by that time the damage is done.

The phone is ringing off the hook. My client wants to know why he has received such a nasty notice about me.

Most people don't understand this complex and often abused system. It is as archaic as anything ever conceived by the legal wizards anywhere. If lawyers had notices of this nature sent out to their clients, that cast doubts as to their honesty and financial responsibility, there would be many more law suites.

I have heard more horror stories about abuses of the Florida Lien Law then I have ever heard about unscrupulous builders.

If there are lien laws in your state, make yourself aware, read them if you have time, but be sure you know in advance about how these laws affect your project.

Licensing:

Some regulatory and licensing agencies have had traditions of painting the construction industry as a collection of the most dishonest people in the business world. No small wonder the public is apprehensive when dealing with people involved in building.

In states where licensing is required the builders must be well schooled and at great expense in order to qualify for state licensing. After thorough investigation and very difficult written examinations, these same agencies grudgingly issue licenses.

At the same time they warn the public that part of the licensing fees collected are to establish a fund to protect people from the malpractice crimes of the construction industry. The wording is reckless, without any regard for offending and tainting the reputations of a vast majority of honest people who choose this field as a lifetime occupation.

Your Attitude: Ticket to a Happy Ending:

We all like those stories with a happy ending. We see movies and read books where this is how things turn out in the end. Our heroes and heroines of these wonderful fictions always manage to survive terrible adversity only to surface unblemished in the end.

The reality is that you can do even better. You do not have to suffer the adversities, if you are aware of what to expect from the beginning. Being well informed is the key. And once the solution is made known to you, the results will be a happy ending for your story too.

Keep Cool, Be Alert:

Let me list five ideas for you to remember that will help keep you out of the pits.

Gather *enough* information in advance.

This is a very positive must. Do your research, investigate all the avenues you feel you need to know in detail. Take your time and absorb the facts. You cannot possibly remember everything, so keep notes on the things that are most important to you. Just refer to the index of this book as a checklist for yourself.

This will make for a good beginning to your project. You will be adequately informed, and know what to expect as the project progresses.

Set your objectives *realistically*.

You can save a good deal of time and money by having a realistic attitude about what you can afford and about what you can get for your money. Nobody in the construction business is going to make a big mistake and not notice. You will not get that great big bargain like Donna P. thought she had.

Anybody who could make that kind of mistake will probably never finish the project anyway. There is no tooth fairy or genie in a bottle ready to bestow a gift of money.

Don't let your *emotions* rule.

It will be important for you to remember that you are involved in a business venture. Being emotional will add a negative effect on everything that happens in your project. The best solution to any problem is to resolve it in a calm businesslike manner.

Anger and bad temperament are contagious. These emotions may very well come back to roost if you are a temperamental person. It will be in your own best interests to be calm and controlled.

Make *firm* decisions after *thorough consideration*.

The old adage 'plan the work and then work the plan' will be a sound slogan for you to adopt. Stick to you original ideas unless something sensational brings *unusual* opportunity. You have made up lists of the most important things you wanted in your new home. You then went through the process of eliminating some of them. Now stick with the ideas you know are good for your project.

Changes will cost money and add time to the construction schedule. I have had indecisive people spend $20,000. on changes that did not add anything to improve on the original idea. They threw money at their indecision, hoping to improve on ideas that were already the highest and best use.

Be *flexible* when opportunities arise.

There *are* unusual occasions when unexpected opportunities arise. This happens most often in one of a kind houses. Sometimes we get lucky and find a situation that was not obvious on the working drawings. I recently found such a circumstance in a house that was in framing stages, and the owner received a big bonus at a true bargain price.

After we had built all the bearing partitions in this house, there existed a perfect structure for a loft. Without any changes or additions to anything structural, it was obvious that by adding some 2x8 floor joists over these partitions, and then putting down a sub-floor, a loft of over two hundred square feet could be gained for very little money. An attractive staircase was added and the finished product was dynamic. A wonderful computer center was created in what would have been wasted overhead space.

The clincher was that this unforeseen bonus room had a cost per square foot that was the topic of conversation at many subsequent cocktail parties.

Stick tight to the *Golden Rule*

You can never go wrong sticking with the most important rule of life. You do not have to be a pushover just because you treat people with kindness and respect. Construction projects are of long duration. You will be exposed to the same people over a long period of time. Sometimes we become impatient seeing the same faces every day. Remember also that the shoe can be on the other foot. Being a pleasant customer definitely has its advantages.

I know if you did all these things with me as your builder, you would be certain of a happy ending to your dream home story.

Closing Thoughts:

Many times throughout my career in the construction field I became discouraged enough to think seriously about doing something different.

Bad economic times, extremes in the financial markets, bank failures, major accidents affecting workers compensation, natural disasters, all had major negative impacts on how my business faired.

These events as they occurred over the years triggered new legislation, layers of new regulations, and sometimes-hostile reactions from government and the public.

Overkill was always the order of the day. Many of the 'new' regulations created greater expense for consumers, but the construction industry took the rap.

My first building permit in Florida took ten minutes to be issued and cost $8. The last one took two months and was over $13,000. That is still hard for me to believe. Imagine! People say housing is too expensive and I had to charge the clients a jumble of fees tacked on by the local county government for the privilege of building a house there.

I'm glad I stuck with it. In the long run it was worth the effort, even with some personal sacrifices.

I'm not talking about financial gain here. I found opportunity in this field that made my daily life exciting. I could hardly wait to get to the construction sites because of my involvement in some of the most challenging of research projects. Helping develop new technologies, methodology, time and cost saving ideas. Just sometimes the pure excitement of seeing the building take shape, become something more than sticks and bricks.

I have met the greatest people I have known in my life. My best friends. So the benefits have been far more that monetary.

My mother told me a long time ago that one of the best things that could ever happen to me in my lifetime is; to love my work.

And so I have.

Pierre Renaldo
March 31, 2000
Roatan, Islas de la Bahia
Republic de Honduras

About the Author

Pierre Renaldo, a semi-retired general contractor, lives on the island of Roatan, the largest of the Bay Islands, thirty-five miles off the North Coast of Honduras. He has written many articles about hurricanes and hurricane resistant structures for several newspapers and magazines in Florida where he formerly resided.

He is author of '**Roatan Insights**', a monthly news e-magazine of information about living/retiring in the Bay Islands, and building your dream home in a third world paradise. He is also editor of '**Coastwatcher**: **Caribbean West**' a weekly newsletter about life in the Bay Islands of Honduras and the North Coast.

Other works by this author:

Non-fiction:
    Felix Prince of Cats and Mitch the Great Storm of the Century
    How to Build Your Dream Home in a Third World Paradise
    How to Survive In Third World Retirement: The Handbook

Fiction:
    Red Dog Chronicles
    Ironshore   The screenplay   (June 2001)
    Ironshore   The novel   (October 2001)

www.ingramcontent.com/pod-product-compliance
Lightning Source LLC
Chambersburg PA
CBHW030355290526
45785CB00004B/1768